THE WIND THIEF

VANISHED, BOOK FOUR

B. B. GRIFFITH

Griffith Publishing

Publication Information

The Wind Thief (Vanished, #4)

Copyright © 2023 by Griffith Publishing LLC

Paperback ISBN: 979-8-9874270-1-9

Ebook ISBN: 979-8-9874270-0-2

Written by B. B. Griffith

Cover design by Damonza

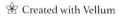 Created with Vellum

To Chris McGrady.
A true family man.

"There is nothing as eloquent as a rattlesnake's tail."

- Navajo Proverb

1

GRANT ROMER

When the sun dips behind the Chuska Mountains to the west, the valley is drenched in amber and just dark enough that I ease off the gas. The roads in this part of the Rez are twisty. It's easy to end up in a ditch, especially at night. My truck can handle pretty much anything. Dad's RV? Not so much. We call it the Old Boat for a reason.

Dad uses the Old Boat as a mobile doc's office. It's been lots of places I never thought it'd make it back from, but still, this is a hell of a place to blow a tire. I keep telling Dad to stick to driving east of the Arroyo, where the New Mexico desert is flat as a pancake. If he's gotta go into the foothills and mountains, he should use his crow totem. But sometimes he don't like to listen.

West of the Arroyo, most of the BIA roads stop and the local roads begin. If you know what you're doing, you can wind your way on the local roads through the bucks and folds of the Jemez Mountains all the way over the Arizona border. That way is dark, with no streetlights to speak of. People drive by sun or by moon, and if they pop a tire on washout scree, they'd better be ready to walk fifty miles to civilization. I had to do it once, when I was sixteen. I was just lucky I had my crow to tell me which way to walk. Out here, if you're on foot too long, you're coyote meat.

Since then I've probably put ten thousand miles of local dirt under my tires, most of them on the west side on account of Kai living out here. I know there's really no *good* place to pop a tire, especially on Chaco Navajo Reservation, but this here is Crooked Snake Road, and Crooked Snake Road is particularly bad. Not just cause of the snakes it's named after neither. Cell service is nonexistent. No mile markers. People gotta be real heads-up about landmarks and know how far 'till the next outpost. Keeping a spare in the truck is smart as well.

What *ain't* smart is taking Crooked Snake in a ten-year-old camper with more miles on it than any three beat-up F-150s on the Rez combined. What *ain't* smart is leaving that camper's twelve-ton bottle jack in the garage back home right next to a crow totem, one that can give you a stride a mile long and get you out of trouble. Those things ought to occur to a man like Owen Bennet, but then again, sometimes Dad ain't all that smart.

Don't get me wrong—he's a brilliant doctor, and he's my dad, and I love him. But when it comes to things like towing capacity, ground clearance, tire wear and the like —basically, anything with an engine—he's kinda lost. I eventually had to revoke his electrical privileges with the wiring on the Old Boat. He already died once. No need for him to push his luck.

My truck is eighteen years old, same as me, but I looked under the hood of a dozen or so before I settled on her, and I've replaced most of the things that get people in trouble out here: belts, breaks, plugs. Shocks too—that's why she glides over the washboarding like she was born for it. Sure, it ain't much to look at, but I'm not trying to draw attention to myself. Most of the Navajo guys—first thing they buy when they get their eighteen money is a truck. I see more brand-spanking new trucks on Chaco Rez than in Albuquerque, even. But with me, it's different. If I was driving around in a new truck, I'd get looks, and when you carry the bell around your neck, you don't really want looks.

My bird is a floating slice of midnight in the distance, the last full rays of the sun reflecting off his feathers.

"He's up ahead," Chaco says.

"Is he alright?" I ask—not out loud but in my head. Chaco and I have an interior dialogue, the way you might talk to yourself, but he answers.

"Seems fine. He's sitting on a rock by the side of the road just up ahead. Looks like he's working some kinks out of his back."

I shake my head. *Owen Bennet, always trying to do too much too soon.* Whatever he has, he gives. He took off for Kai's place as soon as I even suggested something might be wrong with her. Never mind he had only about a seventy-percent grasp on where she lives.

In the back of my mind, I hear Joey Flatwood say, *You knew he would do this. That's why you told him.*

And maybe I did. The bell sometimes shows me things others can't see. And what I see is that Kai Bodrey is sick—with what, I don't really know. But Owen is the single best person on the planet for helping sick people. I know this is true no matter what her brother Hosteen says. I could say the sky is blue, and Hos would spit on the ground and say, "Prove it, *bilagaana*."

I crest a hill and slow to a roll on the downslope. In the

distance, Owen is standing against a scoop carved out of the pink sandstone, looking embarrassed and blinking in the headlights. The shirt-and-tie combo he always wears on house calls is particularly out of place—like he's on a job interview. He has the kind of smooth face that could get mistaken for midtwenties at first glance, but his hair—or lack of it—gives away that he's on the far side of forty. His widow's peak is as sharp as a knife, the golden red starting to fade to more of a dust color. His eyes betray him too. They're a dusty turquoise that remind me of what my grandpa's used to look like

He flags me over with big flapping arm motions, as if I might somehow miss the enormous RV flashing hazards as bright as campfires.

I park my truck and step out. The fine rocks of the road crunch under my boots as I walk around to the bed and pull out the jack.

"An RV jack doesn't do a whole lot of good sittin' in a garage," I say. I dig around in the pocket of my jeans and pull out his worn-leather totem pouch and hand it to him. "Neither does this."

He takes the pouch and tucks it carefully into a pocket then places his hands on his hips. "Alright, okay. I deserved that. Thank you for your help."

I look up at the purpling sky and find my bird wheeling above. "You should thank Chaco. He's the one that saw you laid up."

Owen leans back and cups his mouth then yells, "Thank you, Chaco!" loud enough to echo off the canyon and cause me to cringe. Joey once told me not to yell into the desert at night unless I wanted a response. Chaco lets out three bemused caws anyway.

The flat is on the right rear, which is a double set.

Lucky. If he'd blown one of the front tires, the Old Boat would probably be on its side. I sit down in the dirt and unpack the jack.

"Need help?" Owen asks.

I look at him sidelong, ponder it, and shake my head.

"Nah, you're probably right," he says quickly. "Faster if you just do it."

He resumes his old-man workout on the side of the road, rotating his hips like he's hula hooping, watching me carefully as I feel under the frame to get set up.

I can tell he's embarrassed at having to be dependent on me like this. Sometimes, I think Mom and Dad still think of me like they did when they found me at age eight.

"Found the spare in the back," he says, rolling it over to me. "Careful with your fingers. I don't want you to get crushed."

"I don't aim to get crushed, Dad," I say, sighing.

The pipe-mounted stabilizers come in sets of two. I get the rig lifted on both sides, and I'm spinning off lug nuts when Chaco says someone is coming. On instinct, I turn my head to find him, a streak of black like war paint on a stone mesa glowing in the near distance.

Owen keys in on my reaction immediately. "What's up?"

"Chaco says a truck is coming. Maybe three miles back."

Owen smooths his tie. "Maybe it's the tribal cops. Somebody saw the RV and called in for help."

But the way he says it tells me he doesn't quite believe that. I don't believe it either. Crooked Snake Road isn't exactly on the circuit. The only people that come out here are the Bodreys, people that buy bootleg liquor from the Bodreys, and occasionally, idiots like me trying to get closer to a girl that the Bodreys don't want me anywhere near—one Bodrey in particular, who I'd bet my lucky Stetson is driving that truck.

I swap the tires and tighten the nuts, mind racing. I ain't afraid of Hos Bodrey—not exactly. It's just that I've needed to be not afraid of him for years, and it's tiring. The only break I had from Hos was when he had to do a year of juvie in Albuquerque as some sort of deal Sani Yokana, the chief of police, brokered with his people and the Santa Fe cops after Hos paint bombed a five-hundred-year-old statue and generally raised hell at the Native Market.

I know Sani, and I know part of him wanted to let the state cops haul Hos away for good. The Bodreys have a long history of starting shit. They're hard-line Arroyo folks that split their time between the car camp there and their trading post up Crooked Snake. The bootlegging operation is somewhere way out back too. I ain't ever seen it with my own eyes—Kai won't let me past the trading post when she lets me up there at all—but everybody knows it, Sani too. I asked him why he didn't just let the state take custody of Hos for good, but all he said was he's not in the business of banishing people if he can help it. Too few Navajo in this world as it is, he said.

So Hos came back. And he was not happy about how I'd been spending that year inching my way closer to his sister. Maybe he would leave me alone if I stopped seeing Kai, but I doubt it. And that ain't gonna happen anyway.

I let the jacks down easy, and the RV settles like an elephant in the sand. She'll drive, but she's still too thick for the pass by a good sight. "Take my truck," I say. "Follow Crooked Snake all the way up to the fork with a big tree growing out of a rock. Take a right and follow the road all along the bluff, past where you think it stops. You'll see the Bodrey outpost. If you hurry, you can catch the last light."

Dad looks back and forth between me and where Chaco is cutting his silent way through the air toward us. "What are you going to do?"

I stand up and dust my hands off on my old jeans, more gray now than black. "I'm gonna talk to Hosteen Bodrey."

"You sure that's a good idea, out here and all?" Dad rerolls his sleeves in that precise way of his—three flips of the cuff, like he's prepping for surgery or squaring for an old-timey boxing match—and it makes me smile despite the day getting long.

I know from experience that anyone who pushes Owen Bennet too far usually ends up wishing they hadn't. The man wrestled with Death, after all. True, we're friends with Death. And yes, Dad lost and got tossed back to the land of the living—thank God—but he still wrestled the guy and walked away. Not many can say that.

Chaco swoops in low and flares out to land on the side of the road. I toss Dad the keys. "Figure we can buy you ten, maybe twenty minutes. If you leave now."

I can tell he doesn't feel good about it, but I know he's concerned for Kai, too, after what I told him. I ain't ever seen a seizure before I saw that one with Kai, and it scared the shit out of me. One minute, her legs were draped over mine, fingers threaded loosely while we watched TV, and the next, she was hard as a rubber ball against my side, teeth grinding, eyes rolled, hands turned to claws. She didn't answer, no matter how loud I called for her.

Then, she just came out of it, looked around lost and

started crying. Nothing but a thin drop of blood coming from her nose was evidence it ever happened.

Maybe he reads some of that on my face because he opens the passenger door and grabs his faded black doctor's bag.

"Try for twenty," he says.

My truck skitters dirt out the back as he pulls away. I watch until the switchback hides the taillights, and Chaco and I are alone.

"You ready up there?" I ask.

Chaco flaps his huge wings as he resettles himself on a dinner-plate-sized outjut off the mesa. "I'm not a huge fan of you throwing yourself into this type of thing again and again. Remember what you have around your neck, buddy. It's bigger than you or me."

"It's for Kai," I say. "I wanna make sure she's okay."

"Yeah, yeah, you do it for love," Chaco says. "I've heard that one before."

Kai and I haven't dropped the L word yet. But we're getting close, and Chaco knows it. The sunlight has almost totally retreated out of the sliver of valley we're in, but he's got crow sight, and I know he can see me smiling.

2

OWEN BENNET

Grant's truck handles like a dream compared to the Old Boat. Most everything on four wheels does. I'm at the fork in front of the mesa in no time, but here I slow down, way down. The drop-off to the right of Crooked Snake may be a bluff, but if the tires slip, I'm in for an ugly trip back to the base of the foothills. I'm incredibly grateful that Grant invested in the light bar. The way this desert turns to darkness at the flick of a switch still astonishes me. I stick to the established ruts in the narrow road and cross my fingers that my lights are bright enough to give anyone coming the other way some pause.

I'm not sure why I ever thought I could make it up here in the Old Boat—or if by some miracle I did, how I expected to get back down. I would likely get ten points into my twenty-point U-turn by the Bodrey outpost then go tumbling over the side like a log—either that or just keep going and hope to come out on the other side of the Colorado Plateau sometime next week. And forgetting my crow totem was sloppy. I need to be more prepared than that. Caroline thinks I take too much on myself, but this doctors-on-wheels gig was my idea, and I have to make it work. Sometimes, I feel like it's the only real way I can pull my weight in the family.

My father always said practicing medicine meant nothing if it didn't help the community, if I didn't have a *cause.* Caroline and I left ABQ General years ago, but the mobile clinic is my *cause.* I'm following in a long line of Bennet physicians that way. Every time I pick up that black bag, I feel my grandfather nodding in approval across time. My father nods, too, although he does sniff at the Old Boat and cock an eye at the hard-packed desert, at a bit of a loss. It's about as far from Boston as you can get. That's exactly why I came here, of course.

But existential pressure isn't the only thing driving me onward. It's real pressure too. For one, if I don't start charging for visits soon, I'm likely to be the first Bennet doctor to go broke. The Native Americans are among the most underserved communities in the country when it comes to basic medical care. I had an idea of that when I decided to take up the mobile clinic, but the reality was—and still is—shocking. The lack of education, the fear of modern medicine, the sheer *distance* that has to be covered—and then, just when you think you're starting to make some inroads, you blow a tire. My life in a microcosm.

RV tires are expensive too. At least once a day, I think of all the worthless junk I used to waste money on back in the day because I was bored—the air fryer and nonstick pans off the infomercials, the rare-release bourbon, the massage chair. That damn thing alone would've been two full tanks of gas for the Old Boat.

But charging someone for a house call is hard when I

see the tape holding their sandals together is starting to fray.

The light bar catches something, throwing a sharp shadow out in front of me, and I hit the brakes. The tires slide a bit on the dirt, skittering tiny rocks down the shelf of the bluff. The fork with the tree growing out of the rock —I almost missed it.

I throw the truck into reverse and creep backward, very carefully, and pull in behind the tree, down a bit so that the big rock hides the truck. I kill the engine and grab my bag. When I step out, I'm swallowed by the night.

I start walking. A small light glows up ahead, and I focus on that. Nothing looks out of the ordinary, if you consider a visit to a backcountry bootlegging shack ordinary, but a sound stops me cold, like sand sprinkling on glass. I freeze as a snake sluices across the road in total silence, maybe six feet in front of me.

I'm used to seeing snakes out here, garter snakes, mostly. I've heard a few rattlesnakes doing their thing but have never come across one, thankfully. This is no garter snake or rattler. It's thin and long and banded white and black.

It stops in the middle of the road and turns its bullet-shaped head toward me. A white band crosses its face, too, giving the unsettling impression of a mask.

"Get out of the road, please," I say, only recognizing how strange that sounds once I've said it, as if it might respond to polite manners.

It stares at me, black tongue flicking, and for a terrible moment, I think I'm going to have to try to stomp my way out of this in loafers that show entirely too much ankle. After a moment, it slides its way to the other side, and the little hairs on the back of my neck settle again. The snake must've been caught by the sudden temperature drop when the sun disappeared, to act like that. At least, that's what I tell myself to calm my racing heart the rest of the way up.

Ahead, a simple structure sits against a backdrop of stars, low and flat, maybe twice again the size of the Old Boat, a bit like an improvised double-wide. Two hissing propane lanterns illuminate a single wooden slab of a door. Beyond, the land falls away again, scruffy with mesquite and creosote bushes that fade quickly to darkness.

The Bodrey trading post.

I know surprisingly little about the Bodreys, considering my son is head-over-heels in love with one of them. I can see why Grant likes Kai. She's very pleasant to Caroline and me, but in that twinkle-in-the-eye way that tells me she's got a bit of a fearless streak held back like a trick card up her sleeve. I know that look—know how hard resisting it can be—because Caroline has a bit of it too.

Hosteen Bodrey is an angry young man, militant in his beliefs about protecting what he sees as the old ways of his people. They landed him in jail for a while, and then Grant said he bounced around a bit doing nothing productive. Their dad died while Hos was away, caught in a vapor fire that took out one of their hidden distilleries somewhere in the valley beyond, according to Sani Yokana. The mother, Bly Bodrey, lives here still but is ill. From what Kai described, it sounds like diabetic neuropathy, which makes for a particularly brutal day-to-day, even for an area of the country where chronic pain seems as prevalent as the desert dust.

But I'm not here to see Kai's mother. I'm here to see Kai, and I don't have much time.

I knock sharply three times on the spring-hinge door then step back into the harsh brightness of the propane lanterns. The curtain on the single-pane window to my right flutters, and I see a flash of glossy black hair. When Kai opens the door, I get a waft of fry bread and can almost taste the butter. She's dressed in a black tank top that hugs her chest and dark jeans tucked into ankle boots made of black leather worn nearly white at the heel. She also looks like she might fight me.

"Hi, Kai. I'm just here because Grant asked me to come." Something occurs to me. "Please tell me Grant also told *you* he asked me to come."

I've used the crow totem to phase to some of these backcountry places before, for a drop-in, but explaining away how I showed up out of the blue is always tough. If the Navajo ever caught me phasing in and out, they'd brand me a witch, for sure. Plus, I almost always lose my bag when I try to carry it through.

The way Kai looks out beyond me, scanning the run up to the outpost like she was counting every star, every rock, every roll of the hills to make sure they were in their proper places, makes me very glad I came in the truck.

I jangle Grant's keys in my pocket. "I parked behind the rock tree, like Grant said."

She exhales and mutters Grant's name under her breath in a way that is somehow both reprimanding and strangely endearing. "I don't know how many times I gotta tell him I'm fine," she says. "Get in before someone sees you."

The Bodrey trading post is a bit like a cross between an army surplus and one of those run-down NYC bodegas that are almost certainly fronts. Outside of cigarettes, jerky, and energy drinks of all sorts, what's on offer has very little rhyme or reason. Shovels, buckets, barbed wire, camping equipment, construction vests—it's all a mish-mash of different colors and shapes.

Kai leads me through the back of the shop into a living area that is actually quite cozy. A laptop glows on a low end table, adjacent a small kitchen with an electric stove and a chipped wooden table. Someone snores heavily from behind a narrow door in the back—likely Bly, medicated, and in bed.

Kai bids me sit in the den, and I catch a glimpse of an essay of some sort on the whirring laptop before she closes it. Grant has told me Kai is considering enrolling at UNM in Albuquerque—or maybe ASU—somewhere still near the land of her people but far from her family. I don't blame her. I also don't think this place will survive all that long without her at the front desk. And I have no idea what her mother is going to do without her.

I can see these things, or things very much like them, weighing on her. Her gaze is distant, caught up on a small totem set in the center of the table—a bear sprinkled with what looks like blue cornmeal. I've seen bear totems before but never one carved out of black obsidian and certainly not one with white eyes. I recall the banded snake that seemed to be waiting for me on the road, and for a moment, my own totem feels like it thrums in my pocket.

I pull my black bag around and set it on the table between us, and my world comes back into focus. "Tell me what happened."

"It's not a big deal. Sometimes, I feel really tired—that's all."

She tucks her hands between her thighs, and I wait. My father used to say that silence was one of many tricks of the trade that doctors shared with bartenders. And trust me, he would know.

"I got up in the middle of the night to get a glass of water, and everything went woozy. I sort of... fell. Woke up on the floor by my bed."

I grip the bag more tightly by the worn leather handle and try not to think of Ben Dejooli, collapsing out at the Arroyo way back. "When did this happen?"

"Yesterday."

"Has it happened before?"

Her eye catches mine in a quick flicker that tells me the answer even before she eventually nods. "Once or twice. I eat something and feel better. Sometimes I think I forget to eat. I got a lot on my mind." She gestures at the laptop and the store and glances beyond the little kitchen toward her mother's room and then at the bear totem last of all. Her fingers tremble when she brushes a strand of hair behind her ear. Her brow is damp.

The air thrums. Assigning cosmic significance to that banded black bear is easy enough, after what I've seen over the years, but I still believe fortune favors the rational mind. Medicine does as well. And her aside about feeling better after food strikes me as important.

"What did you eat to feel better after you passed out?"

She seems to wince at the phrase, but that's what happened. She passed out. I tiptoe around a lot of topics in this world, but physiology is not one of them.

"Just some crackers," she says, shrugging. "And orange juice."

I nod and pop open my bag. "Have you ever had a blood workup?"

Kai looks at the worn leather like it's the gaping maw of some monster.

"I take it that's a no. If you'll allow it, I'd like to take a blood sample just to rule some things out."

She looks unconvinced, and I know I'm not going to get another shot at this. "Please, Kai. For Grant, if only to get him off your back about it."

She allows a slight smile. If I were to guess, not a lot of people have cared about Kai the way Grant does. It's a powerful thing, to have someone care about you and to get that care returned. It has a way of softening even hard-luck eighteen-year-olds—cynical physicians, too, and their lovably neurotic nurse life partners.

"How long does it take?" she asks, but she's already scooting closer, holding out one hand, palm up, as if I'm going to take it out of her wrists.

I pull a sample kit and cleaning swab from the bag and set about cleaning the crook of her elbow instead. "Five minutes, max." *If I can get the damn line started*. A good blood draw requires a good jab, something Caroline could do in her sleep. Not me—somewhere in the dusty old book of doctoring, someone decided white coats were above venipuncture, which naturally came right around to bite me in the ass when my practice shrank from being a fellow at ABQ General to being one of two people in a retrofitted RV. Thankfully, Caroline made me practice on her until I was at least serviceable once more.

Then again, she never had me practice when an ex-con was on approach. My hand flutters a bit with the butterfly needle, and Kai sees it. I clear my throat to draw her attention back to my face, say a prayer to whoever is listening, and ease into the vein. I act like it's normal when I hit pay dirt on the first try. Pretenses must be made.

Dark blood shoots through the piping and spatters into the first vial. When it's full, I swap in the second and manage not to turn their den into a murder scene. That's when I hear the angry rumble of a big truck coming around the bend.

Kai jerks her arm, and I almost lose the rig. "You need to get the hell out of here."

"Almost done," I say. "Squeeze your fist a few times."

She pumps a few times and shakes her head. Anxiety creeps over her like a heavy blanket, weighing her visibly. "You sure you parked far enough behind the rock tree? If he saw Grant's truck—"

"Don't worry about the truck." I pop off the second vial and ease the needle out again under a cotton ball. I even prepped the Band-Aid for easy on. Caroline would be proud, but only if I manage not to come home black-and-blue.

I secure the samples and pop off my gloves, tossing them into the bag for good measure. She's up and moving to the back before I can even close the bag.

"You should have a cookie or something. Take it easy—"

She snorts as if the idea is a joke. And maybe it is. She can't exactly lie back on the couch with a cooling mask and a glass of wine and binge-watch shows, order take-out Chinese, and decompress. Kai has never known such things.

"I don't know how you're gonna get out, but you gotta get gone."

I let her escort me out the back door, ducking under as I go. "Don't worry about me. Thanks for allowing the draw. I'll be in touch."

She looks down at me pityingly then closes the door, as if to say, *What's the use?* A pair of headlights cuts the night in the distance. The Bodrey trading post is at the top of the pass, set back in the fold of the hill. Under normal circumstances, I'd be backed up, trapped. But normal circumstances don't apply when you have the crow totem I have.

Time to step back into the phone booth of oblivion.

I set my bag down carefully in the dark fringe of the dirt lot then reach into the worn leather pouch in my pocket and grip the crow around the smooth stone of its belly. I haven't had to use it all that often since the Coyote, but my hand still fits around it like a glove, like it's been waiting.

Reality snaps into a sepia night vision, and I can see for miles even as I drop out of sight. The world whips in a silent sandstorm, as if reality is constantly siphoning itself away but never disappearing. This is the thin place, the infinite crawl space between the land of the living and the land of the dead.

People aren't meant to be here. That much becomes very obvious when the sting starts, a single pinpoint burn like a focused application of liquid nitrogen on a trouble-some spot of skin—except deeper, in my soul. And the longer I stay, the more it spreads.

The thin place has its advantages, though. For one, I can drop out of sight of men like Hosteen Bodrey and his entourage, just now hopping out of a shiny extended-cab truck on huge tires. I look from the simple trading post back to the truck and try to do the math.

Either he stole it, or the bootlegging business must be booming.

Equally as beneficial, however, is the mile-long stride I get as long as I hold the crow. Distance—and time, for that matter—passes differently here. My working theory is that the closer one gets to death, the less things like distance and time matter.

A mere shuffle would take me right past them and to Grant's truck—I could walk all the way back to Grant in a half step—but something stills me. Hosteen is speaking with deference to a man in the back of the cab. He's holding out a hand and helping the man down. From what I know of Hosteen Bodrey, he doesn't speak with deference to anybody. I've since learned that "Hosteen" is an honorific that people around the Arroyo use tongue in cheek when they talk about Hos Bodrey. Navajo humor works that way, from what I can understand. Hos took it regardless and owned it. Seems to be his modus operandi.

The sting isn't too bad yet. Sometimes, I think the thin place takes a second to notice you're there, so I take advantage and ease myself over their way for a closer look, taking care not to step right off the hill. The thin place wants to take you far away, so walking a few steps here and there is tricky. If Hos could see me, he'd likely think I was one of his bootleggers wandered in from the nearest still, too drunk to pick up my feet.

But he doesn't, of course. He can't.

Age is sometimes hard to tell with the Navajo—old men can seem young, and young men can seem old—but the man Hosteen helps down from the truck is a strange mix of both. If I had to guess, I'd put him at sixty, but a strong sixty, with long white hair and skin like oiled leather. They speak in Navajo. I've picked up a few phrases here and there over the years—enough to show gratitude, basically, and ask where it hurts. He's asking about Kai.

The man is blind. That much is evident in the way he looks at the night sky with eyes closed, head softly seeking. His steps are slow but confident as Hos leads him inside.

I follow them to the front door. The burn is stronger now. The tips of my fingers are exhibiting the telltale signs of early frostbite, another charming aspect of the thin place, but I hold tight to the crow totem anyway.

A shuffle to the right takes me through the thin outer wall and back into the Bodrey outpost. Hosteen calls for Kai, and she comes around from the back as though she was watching over her mother all evening. He introduces the blind man in Navajo I can't understand, tracing back the clans in a cadence reminiscent of the begats, and while Kai gives a polite bow at each, the smile she affects seems strained and stops short of her eyes.

Hosteen switches to English. "Speak your greeting, Kai. He can't see you nodding."

Kai clears her throat and stammers, "Welcome, uncle. You've traveled a long way. Let me get you some food and drink."

The man smiles and responds in low, full English as he feels about for the seat behind him. "Call me Jacob. My people call me Jacob Dark Sky. But that is my singer's name. And I have not sung for you yet."

Kai looks sharply at Hosteen, who returns her gaze unflinchingly.

Jacob Dark Sky moves his head in a small tic, as if testing the air between them. His laugh is soft and gentle. "Perhaps I am getting ahead of myself. Let's start with a glass of water."

"I hope you didn't come all the way from California for nothing, Jacob," Kai says. "I've already been to see the Arroyo singers. They've seen nothing wrong. Plus, we don't have the money to hire a singer—"

"The Arroyo singers are old fools," Hosteen says sharply. "And you wouldn't say I'm overreacting if you saw what I see out there in the hills and the valleys. This isn't just about you, Kai. This whole reservation is weak and getting weaker."

Dark Sky holds up a hand, and brother and sister are stilled. His directionless smile cuts the tension between them. "I am sure your singers are not fools. But Hosteen was right to call for me. I am blind in one way, but I see in others. And what I see is a sickness on this place."

Dark Sky reaches out in one fluid motion and picks up the black bear totem from the table with shocking accuracy. When he touches the stone, I see it change.

When I'm in the thin place, the crow totem glows, a bit like when someone puts their hand over a powerful flashlight and it shines through the skin. This is that times ten, like staring at snow reflecting sun. A swirling white burn knits itself around the totem, and for a moment, I'm so stunned that I almost drop my crow.

Thankfully, I gather myself in time to prevent myself appearing from thin air by the coffee table. The sepiascape never breaks. Kai and Hosteen never even blink. This white burn is as invisible in the living world as I am.

But Jacob Dark Sky turns his blind eyes my way.

I fully expect to be called out where I stand and told to step forth and explain myself. Instead, he sets the black bear gently back down on the table. The white burn fades until it disappears.

"A sickness," he says again, nodding. "But of the spirit. I am sure of it."

I don't believe he can see me—at least not fully. His eyes still quest underneath the lids. But he senses something of me, more than any normal man should.

I've had just about enough of this on every level. The pain is getting acute, and that totem looks like it's got Mona Lisa eyes. I shuffle out.

Back in the dark fringe, I let go of my crow. The warmth of the desert night settles over my shoulders like a blanket, and I gulp air as quietly as I can. I'm away from the post but can't tell how closely anyone is listening. With any luck, they'll think the *whoosh pop* was a car back-firing on the reservation road below.

I pick up my bag and take careful steps away, keeping to the full darkness even after the trading post disappears around the bend. Once I'm back in Grant's truck, I click on the battery and flip on the headlights, but I coast in neutral back down the pass for a good long while before firing up the engine.

Back near the turnoff, Grant waves me over. He looks miraculously unmussed despite his eighteen-year-old bravado, all gung ho to go toe-to-toe with Hosteen.

I pull in behind the newly shoed Old Boat and throw the car into park. I'm still flicking away that burn from the tips of my fingers as I step out.

"How'd it go?" we ask at almost the same time.

"You first," I say.

Grant takes off his hat and wipes sweat from his fore-head, looking up the pass behind me. "I sat on the grill out here and waited, saw him coming, even nodded, but he never even slowed." He puts his hat back on and his hands on his hips. "It's the damnedest thing. I know he saw me. But he seemed in a real hurry to get up Crooked Snake. Never even slowed."

"He has company," I say.

"What kind of company?" Grant asks.

"The kind that makes me want to get the heck out of here and talk about it back home."

Grant pops his hat back on and dusts his hands off on his jeans. "So that kind of company, then. Sounds about right, considerin' it's Hos and all, and I don't think he ever kept good company in his life. Except for Kai, of course."

"I've got a theory on her condition as well," I say. "I'll tell you all about it."

Grant hops into the truck, and I hop in the Old Boat, and as I pull back onto the access road toward town, I can still feel the weight of those blind eyes questing after me.

3

CAROLINE ADAMS

About ten years ago, I spent an entire sleepless night eating something between three and five bags of low-cal popcorn and making a list of the pros and cons of staying on as a nurse at the Chaco Health Clinic. To my absolute nonsurprise, it became a list laying out the pros and cons of the two men I was in love with at the time, one of whom was and still is dead.

Believe it or not, things got weirder from there. But long story short, I decided, wisely, to hitch my wagon with Owen, the man I loved who was alive. With each passing year, I'm more and more convinced that I made the right decision although—I'm not going to lie—sometimes, on really dark nights when the sky over the Rez looks like diamonds scattered across velvet and I swear I'm seeing to infinity, I can almost feel him: Ben Dejooli—the Walker, now—and I'd give almost anything just to be able to talk to him again.

That's just silly because I will be able to, one day. You will too. All of us will. That's his job. But I'm not talking about "talking" in a professional capacity. I'd just like to sit with him again and chat about his world and my world and how crazy it is that two people can be a world apart, sitting in the same room.

I dropped that letter of resignation in my supervisor's box at the CHC that day, and I thought I was doing a brave thing, as if quitting the completely overrun CHC and taking their top doctor with me on a mission to restore a cosmic balance would also somehow put an end to the nonstop flow of mid- to heavy-grade suffering that walks in and out of the clinic doors every day.

That was, as our Arroyo friend the Smoker likes to say, "some white-people-shit way of thinking, right there."

Don't worry. He doesn't say it like it's a bad thing, necessarily—more like an inevitable thing, the way someone might shake their head at a puppy chewing on the laundry. And in this case, at least, he's right. Turns out the Navajo need as much help at the CHC as they do out in the field, so now Owen and I split our time doing both. I suppose you could say I sort of unresigned. We're still freelancers, but as far as I can tell, the only real difference is we get paid whenever IHC gets around to it instead of every two weeks.

The Smoker sells what he calls "native cures" at a card table outside the CHC. I'd call it a side hustle, but I think it's his main hustle unless his main hustle is just staying alive at the Arroyo. He sets up at the street corner by the Quik-N-Go, which also just happens to be the requisite one hundred feet from the CHC entrance so that he can keep ripping his cigarettes. Some of these "cures" aren't half bad, actually. The osha root and the piñon-sap salves might help some inflammation. He has some blackberry-root-and-honey mix in old lip balm containers that might not hurt people if it is what he says it is.

Others, I'm not so sure of: dream catchers, smudge sticks, medicine wheels, and various rocks he says have spirit power or whatever. When I look at these, I can't help but hear Owen's voice. *The day I actually observe a smudge stick smudging away cirrhosis, I'll be first in line at that table.* And the medical side of me knows he's right —mostly.

I can actually see the smoke those sticks of sage are supposed to affect. Call it an aura. Call it spectral sight. Call it whatever you want. I see colors coming off of people, and I have a pretty good idea of what they mean. Sometimes I can calm them, too, making them change. Owen is right that a smudge stick isn't going to clear the smoke of a person who's terminally ill, but it does make it move, make it shimmer, give it a little bit of life when it's growing yellow and brittle. Smoke recognizes smoke. The Navajo know that.

I pause at the table, and the Smoker looks up at me as he finishes his Quik-N-Go burrito and plucks a cigarette from behind his ear. He flips it between thumb and fore-finger as naturally as I chew gum.

"*Ya'at'eeh*, paleface!" he says, and by now, I know he means it as kindly as a guy like him can mean it. "Is today the day you finally come around to the true medicine?"

I snort. Unless he's got some anxiety meds mixed in with all those crystals or a pregnancy test in that pack of his, he can't help me. But I'm not about to get into that with the Smoker right now, or ever. Instead, I pick up a clump of pink quartz from the table and look at him with one eye very cocked.

"Crystals? Really? I'm pretty sure that's not even like a Navajo thing. That's a hippie-dippie thing."

"Where you think the hippies got it?" he asks, stirring

the pile with his yellowed fingernail. "All I know is I've seen rocks do strange things."

He looks at me for what feels like a minute but is likely just a few seconds, and my crow totem suddenly feels heavy in my pocket. Sometimes, I feel the entire reservation knows about the Circle and what the crow totems can do and how it's our job to protect the Keeper, to protect Grant, to protect the bell and protect the balance.

Then he coughs generously into his elbow, which I appreciate, and the look is gone. "And even if they ain't shit, I got the whole sack of them from my auntie who picked them up for pennies at an estate sale in Gallup. A man's gotta make a living, right?"

Funny how even his benign smile—the way he talks straight to me—makes me feel more like a part of this place than anything I do to patch up the same people that come in and out of the CHC revolving door. Don't get me wrong—it's gotta be done—but the Rez can make people feel very lonely. Crazy how you can feel alone even when you're with your family. Owen, Grant, and I—lonely together.

Joey does his best to bring us in to the Navajo community, but he can only do so much. Ben used to help bridge that gap, too, but he's been MIA. Grant's the only one who could really ask after him, through Chaco, but Chaco has been pretty quiet on the subject of Ben lately, and I'm a little afraid to ask why. Every time I do, I get cryptic answers from the bird, like *It's hard work being Death,* or the worst, *I wish I knew.* Chaco knows everything. Or he should.

I put on a smile. The Smoker doesn't need to see behind the curtain. I like talking to him on my way into work, but that's where it needs to stay.

"Just promise me this," I say. "If someone comes up to you with a gunshot wound or, like, pale and inches from collapsing, don't sell them some crystals. Tell them to cross the street and come on into the clinic. Can you do that?"

The Smoker takes a drag and sniffs as if that's some huge ask. "Fair. I don't want anyone collapsing at my office. Bad for business." He lifts one corner of his mouth one millimeter, which is how I know he's joking.

I wave my way through a cloud of cigarette smoke to cross the street. "So is that a no on the pink crystal?" he calls after me. "How about I just put it on hold, then?"

Inside the CHC, the emergency intake is as packed as an inner-city bus station at rush hour, but without all the charm. People sit side by side lining the walls and back-to-back clumped in the middle. The place is roiling in the type of smoke only I can see, the color of discomfort, fear, pain. It wafts across the space in brown and gray like a gust of wind kicking up grit in a dirty alley. I've seen the CHC full before, and no emergency room is ever going to have what you might call *good* vibes, but I'm having a hard time thinking of the last time it had this kind of smoke in it. I can't quite remember when it started to get this bad, but it feels like the smoke gets heavier every week.

I move over to the front desk, where our longtime intake secretary, Dee, looks spooked, like she's wandered into the wrong building.

"Glad you're here. This place is full moon wild today," she says, turning to her yellowed computer. Her press-ons clack each key like it's a typewriter. "Schedule has you starting in Room Five. Don't forget to clock in."

I take the schedule off the tray of our ancient printer and move through the door into the back to key in my contractor ID. The alley haze is here too. Dirty smoke like the end of a fireworks show floats through the halls and seeps out from the exam rooms. Dr. Sadler, one of the few full-timers, presses past. I can smell stale sweat on him, nervous sweat. Dr. Sadler is never nervous. He's been here for so long that I have no idea what his actual specialty is, not that the clinic is exactly picky. When it gets busy, everybody is a generalist.

"One of those days," he says, looking at me and twirling a forefinger around his temple. "Any chance you could call Owen in? I think we're gonna be in for a long night, otherwise."

"He's on a house call," I say. "But I can give him a ring once he gets back in service."

Sadler lets out a breath that tells me all I need to know, then he's off, waddling in his baggy khakis faster than I've seen him move in months.

I pluck out my phone and give Owen a call, suddenly wanting to hear his voice. He was always good in these situations back at ABQ General, and I think Sadler is right. Whatever is going on here, he needs to know about it.

The call goes straight to voice mail, of course.

"Hi, honey. Hope things are going okay with Kai. If you have any gas left in the tank, I think you should come to the clinic. It's... hazy in here. If you know what I mean. Weird hazy."

I hang up and take a deep breath, already feeling the stress sweat prickling my armpits. A decade doing this, off and on, and I still sweat more than I'd like to admit whenever I look at a packed schedule. And then, of course, the sweat makes me cold, which makes me tense, which makes me sweat more. It's a fun thing I do.

I gently knock on the door to Exam Room Five in that perfunctory way that says I'm coming in either way, and we're off.

THREE HOURS and nine twenty-minute patient slots later, my eyes are burning, and I've got that pinched feeling, like from a ponytail that's too tight. But it's all over me. I've got tight-ponytail body.

I pause in front of my next exam room and take a quick second to try to mentally talk my anxiety down. I haven't felt this piled on at work since my days on the oncology floor, and it's coming back at me a bit like PTSD. Whenever I used to get like this at ABQ General, I would take a bathroom break and drink some water. Grant drinks tons of water. He has a whole jug in his truck. He was horrified when I told him I've gone entire eight-hour shifts too busy to take even a sip of water. I told him to try being a floor nurse. We stop getting horrified pretty soon, of pretty much everything.

My next patient can wait five minutes.

The staff bathroom on the emergency floor of the clinic isn't exactly a place of respite, but at least it's got an air freshener, some room to sit, and a solid lock. As soon as the bolt clicks home, I feel a bit lighter. I check my phone, see a text from Owen that says, "Be there soon," and feel lighter still.

I remember now why I left floor nursing. What I can't quite remember is why I threw myself back into it with fewer resources and more crow's feet around the eyes.

I hear Owen in my head again. *"It's the people. The Navajo."*

And he's right, of course. Between the time I enter an exam room and the time I leave, I know I've quieted some smoke, which gives me just enough of a spark to move to the next exam room. But I also know that "just enough" can keep someone going right up until the day it doesn't. And that, my friends, is what you call burnout. The CHC is ground zero for burnout, especially for people like Owen, who will bleed themselves dry if you let them.

With a second to breathe, I take stock of how oddly similar each patient has been, one to the next. Their symptoms may vary—fatigue, stomach issues, nerve pain, quite a few fainting spells—but I know by the smoke that something similar lies beneath all of them. It's no secret that rez life is no picnic, but weariness seems to be seeping into folks' spirits these days.

I tap idly at the leather totem bag in my pocket. Something about today has the feel of the crow side, the thin side. And if that's the case, only a few of us can do anything about it.

A pang of nausea brings me back to the present, where I'm still holed up in a bathroom, sitting on a toilet. *Charming.* My next patient has been waiting too long. I brace myself to get up, and my eyes fall on all the boxes of toiletry supplies we hide back here to replenish up front. It's donated stuff, mostly—condoms and hand sanitizer and tampons and little packets of ibuprofen—which Dee puts in the front bathroom in little batches because otherwise they get grabbed by the handful, teenage-trick-or-treater style.

One of those things is a pregnancy test. We have boxes of them here. I could take ten and nobody would notice.

Of course, all I would really need is one. Funny how that is. Whenever Dee restocks up front, the pregnancy tests are always the last standing. Condoms go first, which I'm all for. Ibuprofen next. Pregnancy tests last. We've had a few theories on that here. One is that condoms and ibuprofen are repeat goods, things people need again and again. But a pregnancy test? Taking ten tests after that first one wouldn't make a woman any more or less pregnant. She's done the thing. It's written in stone. Or in pee on a little stick, as it were.

The second theory is that a lot of women just don't want to know. For whatever reason—and most of them are probably tragic here, let's be honest—they just don't want that on their plate. The plate's full up with all sorts of other stuff that also sucks, so this sucky thing can wait in line.

And right now, I could be put in that camp. Not the "tragic" part—just the part with the full plate.

Still, I grab one and tuck it into a pocket before I let my mind catch up with what I'm doing. That's another old nursing trick that seems to have jogged loose today— sometimes, people can make their bodies do things they don't want to do if they do them quick enough that their minds can't catch up.

Is that a healthy way to live? Probably not. Is it necessary when wiping asses and inserting catheters and, in general, helping people limp along for a living? You bet it is.

I leave the bathroom, somehow feeling more fragile than when I went in, which isn't a good sign, and when I open my next exam room, I find Owen Bennet already there. He turns to me with that unique, well-water-blue smoke of his wisping off his shoulders, still and calm and as aquiline as his eyes, and I'm reminded instantly why I love him.

The patient here is another young woman with the same sickly smoke.

"I've got this one," Owen tells me, and although I can tell that he's tired and, by the rare smudges of dirt on his usually immaculate oxfords, he's been all over the Rez. But when he smiles at me, I feel like I can breathe for the first time all night.

I hope my eyes say as much as I nod and back out the door. I have another patient—there's always another patient on days like this—but first, water. Be like Grant. The tap is next to the coffee. The coffee is awful. The tap water is awesome.

Go figure.

I'm SITTING with Owen in the CHC staff room, which is about the size of the waiting room in any oil-change shop and shares most of the smells. He's actually drinking the coffee, fearless man that he is. Maybe it's just a survival tactic at this point. Either way, he's pulled his tie down a smidge and unbuttoned his collar, which I long ago learned means Owen Bennet is on the verge of falling asleep standing, but his Yankee work ethic refuses to let that happen.

We've been together long enough that we can sit side by side without saying a word and still have a conversation. On days like this, I'm reminded of how lucky I am to have that.

Owen is staring at nothing in particular on the scuffed vinyl floor when he says, "Remember when we used to meet in the break room at ABQ General like this?"

I smile at the memory. "More like I'd wait until I knew

you had a break between patients, and then I'd 'happen to run into you.'"

His laugh is tired but true. "And I'd wait until I saw you there before I took any break." He rubs at his eyes with a forearm, true doctor style—no face touching. "You know, there's a world in which we may never have met."

"Except for Ben," I say. It's out of my mouth before I know it.

We've gone months without talking about Ben Dejooli, months without feeling the need to. Because he's gone years without reaching out to us. We can speculate on where he's gone only so long—the material gets stale.

As big as our jobs are, I know his is infinitely bigger. I can't expect him to be around us much, especially with our history, but the last time I felt even a whisper from Ben was four years and eight months ago. I could feel him lingering after a young Navajo boy bled out here from injuries when his idiot friend rolled a truck racing on IRR9. I felt him then, like a breeze on the back of my neck, but not since. And people have died in the time between. Maybe he's doing the touch-and-go version of things now. Who knows?

For a minute, I think Owen might somehow be hurt. He used to have a bit of an inferiority complex when it came to Ben. But Owen doesn't seem to care. Eventually, he nods in agreement.

"Except for Ben," he echoes.

Sometimes, I forget Owen could miss Ben as much as I do, in his own way.

"I had twenty patients today," I say. "Nine of them had lost time, fainting, or passing out."

Owen nods. "Same with me, more or less."

He somehow saw nearly as many patients as I in a

little over half the time and all with maybe a twentieth of the visible sweat under his armpits.

"I took a blood sample from Kai before I got chased out of the Bodrey place. Ran it down with the lab tech upstairs. She's got all the markers of a diabetic."

Of course. That would explain a lot of what Grant described about Kai's listlessness and the fainting spells, even seizures if her blood sugar got too low. But Owen says this without any sense of victory in diagnosis. I set aside for a moment the way he just dropped in "chased out of the Bodrey place" because it's looking more and more like he and I need to have a sit-down about the things we've both seen over the past twenty-four hours.

"Makes sense," I say. "Give her some fast-acting insulin, get her a glucose monitor. If you teach her how to take care of herself, she'll be right as rain."

Owen makes an exceptionally noncommittal noise even as he nods. "Maybe."

That's all he has to say. He may not see smoke, but he understands that something more is going on here. People seem drained, tired on the inside. There's no quick fix for the harsh side of Rez life.

He leans against me, and I lean against him.

"We'll figure this out," I say.

He allows himself one minute. I know only because I'm watching the old wall clock tick, its white face gone yellow, the second hand as red as blood.

After that minute, Owen straightens his tie, sits up into a slouch, and sips his coffee with a grimace. "Let's finish this day out, shall we?"

He holds out a hand and helps me up.

4

GRANT ROMER

I don't get looked at much, walkin' around the Arroyo these days, and I take that as a good thing. My acceptance here, such as it is, sort of went like this: first time I came through those battered and rusted horse gates set out in the middle of nowhere, separating the dirt of the Arroyo from the dirt of the rest of the Rez, I was fourteen years old. Mom, Dad, and I came up on this place in the dead of night, and I was too young to be afraid even when the Smoker told us to turn around. For one, we were desperate for help only the Arroyo elders could give —on the hunt for a skinwalker, our lives turned upside down—for another, I had my bird.

Since that first visit, the place sort of got a hold of me: the way the rutted road magics itself together at the gate, the dirt packed basically to concrete over the decades. How the people who live here—the poorest of the poor Diné for miles around—still manage to add personal touches to their car camp or tent or lean-to. An herb box here. A wind chime there. Bright-red rain boots in a neat row outside an Airstream that looks older than the hills around it. Crow feathers tied to strips of dried sinew, fluttering in the wind like leashed pieces of the night sky.

Mom and Dad sometimes have a hard time getting past the shady side of this place. It's not huge, but it is there—mostly boosted catalytic converters, stripped wiring, and the like, plus the drugs and booze. If you don't go lookin' for it, it won't go lookin' for you, but they still wouldn't let me near the place alone for years, no matter how many times I asked, not until Joey Flatwood came back.

After his banishment was revoked, he moved back in with a vengeance, right next to the elder brothers Tsosi and Tsasa. He drove his thirty-year-old Suburban to a spot that had been cleared for him, threw it in park, and never started it again. That's probably a good thing because I remember how it hacked its way through those gates that first day. I think it knew it had one last big trip in it, from his exile to his return, then it sat down like an old wolf and gave up its ghost. He anchored it with cinder blocks, swapped the tires for old wooden barrels, and gutted the interior to make himself what you might call an Arroyo studio apartment.

Mom and Dad were okay with me visiting the Arroyo as long as Joey was there. And Joey made a point of always being there whenever I asked if I could come by and grill up some backstrap or roast some good ol' Hebrew National hot dogs over the fire while the elder brothers told stories. At first, I had to have Joey translate every word. Then some time passed, and soon I was only asking for every other then maybe one or two here or there.

Now, I go lots of places Mom and Dad don't know about. I've been fixing up cars across half the Rez and hunting for parts across the other half, but they're still squirrelly about me coming here without Joey, even ten years later.

They might be happy to hear that I'm still a little uncomfortable too, even with my bird perched on my shoulder the way he was that first day.

Joey's place is easy to spot. For the past year, he's been working on painting what I humbly believe is the most badass custom design in the Four Corners region, on the side of his Suburban. A crow spans the entire length of the car, dripping in the colors of a New Mexico desert sunset, eyes a black so deep they look lacquered.

When I walk up, he's going over a wing tip carefully with an old brush. Two flags flutter on a pine-wood pole over his head: a threadbare and faded flag of the state of New Mexico, the sunburst emblem tagged with some graffiti he won't translate for me no matter how much I ask, and above that, an equally faded flag of the Navajo Nation homeland—the Diné Bikeyah—framed between the four sacred peaks.

Makes sense that no one flag would really capture this place. The people who live here are certainly a part of all these places, but they're also a little world unto themselves.

Joey never stops his slow, careful painting even as he says, "She's out back with the twins."

I pause at the border of his camp, where four rocks mark the four cardinal directions, flat things the size of dinner plates dusted with corn pollen. "How is she?"

Joey carefully sets his brush back on the chipped plate at his knees. He stands and wipes his hands off on his oil-stained canvas workpants. Joey is tall for a Navajo, almost as tall as me. But where I have what might be generously called ropey strength, he's thick. Chaco tells me Joey was smaller not all that long ago. The word he used was "diminished." That was back when he was trying to make sense of the bell I wear around my neck and the crow he wears in a leather totem pouch around his. Back when he was trying to make sense of how a little girl he loved like a sister could just disappear. The tribe blamed him. So did Ben. But he fought through. He knew otherwise.

"Hard to say," he says and nods at Chaco in a silent greeting that I feel the bird return with a bob of his head. "One minute, she's fine, chatting like family, working the kettle grill like she was born to it. The next, she's... not there. Distant. She says she just needed a place to rest, but that was hours ago. She just woke up even though the sun is high in the sky."

Chaco chirrups low but says nothing, sort of like a bird grumble.

Tsosi and Tsasa live in the double-wide next door to Joey. They're the kind of old that rumors are made of, but they can still move about and love to hold court at their firepit out back, at the lip of a drop-off where, at night, the stars seem to touch the ground. A woman named Maya takes care of them. She's not related, but here, you don't have to be related to be family.

Joey nods toward their camp, but his eyes are distant, caught somewhere on the thin horizon line. He's been as quiet as my bird recently. I shake my shoulder to give Chaco some life, like he's a clip-on toy, but he just moves and settles again with me, watching along the same line of sight as Joey.

Across the Arroyo, about one good football throw away, an old camper van is packing up. A woman is cranking away at a tattered overhang, bringing it down with a rusty squeal. The man she's with kicks out tire stops that look dug into the fine Arroyo dust like ticks. Their old truck is running but has a bad belt rattle.

"The White River folk are packing up?" I ask.

Joey nods slowly.

"How long they been here?"

"Long time."

Chaco chirps at my shoulder. "Those two, twenty years. But there's been at least one White River at the Arroyo for over a hundred. Until now."

Joey can't hear Chaco, but he exhales slowly through his nose as if he gets it all the same, his jaw tense. "A strange wind blows through the Arroyo these days, Grant Romer." He steps in closer, smelling of paint and sage smoke and clean sweat. "Has the bell spoken to you?"

I thumb it over my shirt and lift it up and off me a bit, out of habit. Usually, if things are acting up between the lands of the living and the dead, the bell reacts in some way. It gets either hot or cold. Sometimes, it feels more real. Nothing like that has happened recently, but I'd be lying if I said I wasn't *noticing* it more and more. It's not heavier, really—just somehow tighter around my neck even though it's on the same woven leather it's hung from for years.

"Hard to say."

Joey nods as if he expected as much. The slamming of a car door echoes across the pit between, and at almost the same time, a chunk of dirt at the lip of the White River camp crumbles down the steep side of the Arroyo there.

Now that I see it, the Arroyo is crumbling at lots of places around the lip, mostly by empty campsites. I can't remember if this many plots were empty before.

"Come," Joey says. "They are expecting you." He opens

the little swinging back gate and holds it for me. "I will return shortly."

"Where you goin'?"

Joey pulls his long hair back and ties it with a beaded strip of leather that glitters black in the sun. "I need to consult with the Circle."

With one last look at Chaco, he ducks into the back of his camper, reaches into his totem pouch, and snaps out of sight.

I look at Chaco. "What was that all about?"

Chaco walks across my back to the other shoulder then turns around again, the bird version of pacing. "This place has a permanence, the Arroyo most of all. When things change here, it's like a canary in a coal mine— which, by the way, is a phrase birdkind do *not* like. Joey thinks all things are connected. And he's got a pretty good track record when it comes to being right about this stuff."

"Permanence? It's a car camp. People are always coming and going. Half of this crowd are junkies."

Chaco pauses and looks at me from an inch away. "And the other half? I have a bird's-eye view, a very old one. There used to be a pattern to the coming and going. But lately, the balance is all out of whack..." He looks into forever away, the way only a crow can. "Remember when we dealt with thin places, way back? The Arroyo is the opposite of that. It has roots that go deeper than you can see. Roots that prop up a lot. Get it?"

"The longer I wear this thing around my neck, the less I get."

Chaco's laugh is a hollow clicking sound that should be as scary as hell but is actually kinda catching. "Talk to Kai. Whatever's happening, I feel like it's happening around her."

I wait for more, but that's all Chaco says. Instead, he just bobs a little, strangely impatient for a thing that's been around since the dawn of time.

Kai sits in a rusted lawn chair underneath a canvas tarp by the firepit out back. A smoldering bundle of sage floats thin wisps of smoke that twist and turn before being snatched away by the cross-canyon breeze. The Smoker is leaning against the fence, wrapping a second sage bundle carefully, unlit cigarette dangling from his lips. The elder twins sit to either side of Kai, dressed in layers of flannel in that way the really old do, no matter what the temperature. She glances up as Maya announces me to the brothers. She looks spacey, like she's half asleep and still trying to place herself. Eventually, she allows a smile. When I first saw her that day back when we were in high school, I wanted nothing more than to have that smile hit me every day. We've been together for years now, on the low, and it still feels brand new every time, even if the rest of her looks dog tired.

"I been tryin' to get a hold of you," I say.

"Hos has too," she says, "which is why I left my phone at home."

The way we're talking through sage smoke lends the whole conversation a strange, dreamy quality. Whatever rest she aimed to get here, it wasn't enough.

"Plus," she adds, "you can always find me if you really want to. You got Chaco." She gives my bird a wink that flutters his plumage a bit.

Kai knows about Chaco and me and the bell. She doesn't quite get it, but she believes it. Course, it's kinda hard *not* to believe when the same bird's been flying in the skies above us for years now.

I take a seat in an ancient folding chair that looks like

it saw its last tailgate before I was born. I pull out an insulin pump and what Dad called a continuous glucose monitor from my dusty road bag. "I brought you something. Dad says it'll help."

Kai looks at all the gear in a daze. "Okay..." she says, drawing it out.

I expected her to be wary. She's old school in a lot of ways, but it's a big thing to drop on someone, that they have a condition they'll need to work on their whole life, one that could kill them otherwise.

"So that's one opinion," she says, allowing it.

"He thinks it's Type 1. Diabetes hits indigenous people pretty hard, in their twenties, usually. He said you could have it without even knowing it. Nothing you've done. He'll come by and teach you how to use it. Set it and forget it. Sorta."

I'm rambling, and I know I've said too much too fast, but I don't know how else to do it. I want to add that I'll be there every step of the way, helping her, that we can do this together—forever, if she wants. But I think that might be *way* too much.

She rubs at her brow. "I'm still getting a second opinion."

"Dad's usually right about this stuff—"

She shakes her head. "Not from a doctor. From a healer. From the brothers."

Tsosi and Tsasa look up at me, their faces inscrutable, pinched with age. So that's why she's here. She's getting the second opinion right now.

I clear my throat, feeling a bit stupid. "You want me to leave?"

Kai focuses hard on her hand, looking at it like it's a stranger's. She seems to be strugglin' to keep it still. When she lets out a breath, relaxing even a little bit, her hand starts to tremble. It's nothing crazy, but it's there, almost like she's shivering, but only in her left hand.

"Not unless you want to," she says quietly.

I manage to stammer out, "Never. I never want to. Leave, I mean."

I would probably say more, but thankfully, Tsosi nods assent in a way that settles me back in my chair.

Tsosi turns to Tsasa and says something in low, slow Navajo that I don't catch. Tsasa grunts in response and pumps at the inner coals of the fire with a tattered bellows, using his stocking feet. The sage puffs white and strong, watering my eyes. If this is what I think it is, they're going to try to diagnose if she's a hand trembler. If she is, then it opens up a whole can of worms. That's an affliction but also a power. Tremblers diagnose tremblers, but they also cure them. If they don't catch it in time, it becomes a dangerous power—an illness, not a gift. She might need a healing ceremony, maybe a Mothway or something, which takes time and means lining up the hogan and the singers and getting together some cash—cash none of us really have.

I take a breath to stop the downward spiral. *One step at a time.* Slow ain't necessarily bad, if it works. Like fixing a flooded engine.

The smoke is thick as Tsasa gestures for Kai to move her chair closer and holds out a hand. That's when Chaco moves on my shoulder, ticking his head at a tiny angle as if catching a sound too high for the rest of us.

"What is it?" I ask, mind to mind.

Chaco puffs up and settles again, teetering his head back and forth. "Hosteen is coming," he says.

"You kiddin' me?" *Talk about terrible timing.*

Chaco turns toward the gate then stills. "I can hear that truck of his a mile away."

I dodged running into Hos out on Crooked Snake, and I could probably do it again. But that's not what Joey would do. That's not what my gut tells me to do neither.

"Well, hell. Guess this is happening."

"What's happening?" Kai asks, watching her hand as Tsosi takes it gently in both of his.

"Looks like your brother is stopping by. And my guess is he ain't here out of love."

Kai takes her hand back. "I thought I had more time," she says softly.

In the quiet waft of smoke, I can hear the truck approaching. The Smoker is looking everywhere but at us and puffing on his cig like there's no tomorrow.

Kai stares daggers at him. "You called him, didn't you."

"He told me to," the Smoker says around his cigarette, tying and retying a sage bundle that doesn't need it, still refusing to meet her eye. "I mean, you know how Hos is. Plus..."

"Plus what?" she asks, with a bit of that old fight in her.

"Plus, he said if I helped him, Jacob Dark Sky would help me."

He crushes some of the sage and sprinkles it at his feet then clears his throat with a cough, which might be a bit more than just a cough, the way I'm seein' things now.

The elder brothers turn their inscrutable look his way, and he flinches. "Look, all I'm saying is I've heard some things about what this guy can do. If what you've got in that arm is bad magic, maybe he can help you too. And fast. Faster than a whole Mothway sing."

The hungry rumble of Hos's look-at-me engine is as

clear as day now, and sure enough, a brand-new truck lifted to hell and back turns in off the access way, pulling around the open fence and cracking a few boulders scattered there, as if to prove a point. Hos sees me and is shaking his head before he even throws the beast into park, his mouth already runnin' as soon as his boots hit the dirt.

"You lost, bilagaana?" he asks. That's Diné for *outsider*.

I ain't gonna lie—that still stings.

Hos went west for a while, doing God knows what, so I ain't seen him face-to-face for a bit. He's bigger than I remember. Though not as tall as me, he's got a lot more meat. He started lifting in juvie then just kept it goin' out there at the trading post with cinder blocks. His hair is long and braided like Joey's, which annoys me for some reason—that he should have that same look—but it's only down to his shoulders. He's got a thick gold chain that pops against his black T-shirt. His jeans and boots look as new as the truck.

He hops the fence into the elder twins' backyard without so much as asking, totally ignoring Maya at the front door. He pulls up just short of me, about one big crow's length away. That isn't a coincidence. He's always pulled up short, so far. He gives Chaco an evil look but leans back when Chaco turns the full power of his side-eye on him.

"How come that thing ain't died yet?" he asks.

"Good to see you too, Hos."

He spits on the dirt and ignores the tut-tutting of Tsosi as he turns to Kai. "You still letting this white boy sniff after you? I thought I said that was over."

Kai looks at me, and for two terrible seconds of eternity, I think she's gonna say she's got no idea what I'm doing here. She might let the past three years of us meeting whenever we could, wherever he wouldn't see us—all of it—blow away like the sage smoke on the wind.

But a half beat before my heart cracks open, she tells him, "I was gonna tell you. Just never seemed like the right time."

Hos flexes his bunched fists and looks at the elder twins for the first time. "Ain't been here in a hot minute. Place looks different, uncles," he says in English before switching to Diné. "Things have changed." He holds out his hands as if to encompass the Arroyo, Kai, me, Chaco, all of it.

Tsosi sighs heavily where he sits, his unblinking gaze boring into Hos. "Things always change," he says in Diné I can barely make out. "But we've seen this kind of change before."

"Then why don't you do something about it?" Hos snaps back in English. "You're supposed to be healers, medicine men. This place is sick. Look around you. Is it any wonder people are leaving?"

Hos spits again, but this time, the elder brothers don't tut-tut—they watch him with those flat gazes, and Tsasa mumbles something I can't catch, something about them not expecting a man like Hos to understand.

Hos gets it. For a second, I think I might see a thick-headed juvenile delinquent assault two old men, but instead, he shifts his hatred back to me and sizes me up again before turning on his sister, as if trying to see how I could even be associated with her. For what it's worth, I sometimes feel that way too, but for different reasons.

She tries to hide her hand, and he picks up on it in a blink. "Lemme guess. You came here asking about that tremble. Then the old men sat around looking at the sky, talking nonsense while that idiot blew smoke at you."

The Smoker looks affronted, but his voice comes out as meek as I've ever heard him. "The old ways have power," he says.

Hos takes a few steps toward the Smoker, who backs up against the fence, trying to make it look purposeful. "Oh, I believe in the old ways," Hos says, "but you ain't gonna find any power in the Arroyo. Not anymore. Come on, Kai. We're going."

Kai stuffs her hands into her pockets and looks down at the smoldering sage.

"Kai, I've been patient. Don't push me."

I take a breath to speak, Chaco tenses his claws on my shoulder, but I say what I wanna say anyway. "She ain't a little girl anymore, Hos."

Hos slowly turns my way, and I can't help but notice the scars on his knuckles. He spits on the ground again and steps up to me, and Chaco tenses in that way that means he's about to launch, but before he does, Maya opens the back door, turns, and shuts it with a slam that catches everyone's attention. She takes off a sandal, gripping it loose and dangerous, like a gangster might hold a 9mm.

"Hosteen Bodrey, if you spit in my backyard again, I'm gonna slap you right out of the Arroyo. What would Bly think, you coming here with such disrespect?"

That gives him pause. He turns back to me and only flinches slightly when Chaco snaps his beak at him with the sound of a popgun. For a second, I think my bird has pushed him over the line, but before he can do anything stupid, Kai stands.

"Enough. This is ridiculous. Fine, Hos. If it gets you out of here, I'll go."

When she passes me, she grasps my arm and leans against me just for a second, then she's away. But in that second, I feel like I've won the whole day. Hos could punch me in the face on his way out, and I'd still feel like I won.

All the same, I count myself lucky that he doesn't.

Aside his truck, he pauses and points at the elder twins. "You want to see the power of the old ways?" he asks. "Come to the flat just past the trading post tonight. Maybe you'll remember what it means to be Diné."

He spits again, but I notice it's very intentionally on the pounded dirt path outside the twins' campsite. "Or keep sittin' here by the fire, watching the Arroyo fall apart around you. Makes no difference to me."

He hikes back in the cab and slams the door. The engine roars as he makes a wide turn and rumbles off. His words linger long after he's gone.

"What's out back of the Bodrey trading post?" I ask.

The Smoker looks down at his sage for a moment then gets back to his weaving with a sigh that rattles his throat. "Some sort of hogan, is all I heard. Dark Sky set it up."

I ask what's been on my mind since the moment I rolled up. "Who the hell is Jacob Dark Sky?"

Maya is still holding her sandal in her hand. The way she stares at the spot Hos left makes me completely certain she was ready to leave a mark with it if she had to. And the way he flinched, it wouldn't have been the first time.

"Hos came back with him," she says. "Rumor is he's some holy man from the Colorado Creek reservation out in California."

The Smoker clears his throat and stares into the fire, scratching at his neck. He looks about as ashamed as I've seen him. But I know how much he cares for the twins, and for him to throw in with Hos over them means he's either in a lot of pain or he's pretty scared. Either way, I'm having a hard time getting angry at him.

Chaco glances over at me. "Jacob Dark Sky is no Colorado Creek Navajo."

"You know him?" I ask, mind to mind.

"Not sure yet. Maybe Hos found him in Colorado Creek, but that's not where this guy came from. He reminds me of someone, but I can't quite figure it yet."

I follow his unblinking gaze to where a banded lizard is slowly raising itself from a rock as the last strong rays of the day slip down the face of the Arroyo. The Rez has lots of lizards, but this ain't any common whiptail. Its eyes flash as it looks our way, two black beads in a stripe of white. The bell thrums against my chest, enough to prickle the back of my neck.

Chaco snaps at the lizard with same popgun retort he shot at Hos, but it doesn't flinch at all. It just looks at us with that ice-cold gaze. Then it skirts the shadows until it disappears down a hole by where the Arroyo is crumbling, completely unfazed.

Wish I could say the same of myself.

5

OWEN BENNET

Caroline isn't sleeping well. I know because I'm also not sleeping well, and whenever we don't sleep well, we tend to do it together. We still sleep on the king mattress I had at my apartment in ABQ, which was lovely when I got it ten years ago, but it creaks like a rusty pogo stick these days at the slightest movement on either side. When one of us wakes up, the other does too. I've been meaning to replace it, but the money keeps going out the door on the mobile clinic, and the rate of replacement is a little lacking, to say the least.

I think of that Albuquerque apartment a lot. I rented it sight unseen because it was on the side of the city that allowed a straight shot to the Rez while still being close to ABQ General. When I first stepped inside, I was fresh off my family's estate in Concord, ready to make a mark. I remember thinking it was small and outdated.

What a snob I was, thinking I was *gutting it out* in a fully furnished two-bedroom-two-bath apartment with an elevator straight to the parking garage. I didn't know what "outdated" was then, but I sure as heck do now.

Our home on the Rez was a picture-perfect definition of both small and outdated when the IHS first put us here years ago once we committed to the CHC contracts. We've improved it noticeably since then, or rather, I improved it marginally then Grant improved it noticeably once he came into his own with a box of tools.

Our bedroom is on the ground floor. Grant has the loft, to which he added an outdoor ladder so as not to disturb us with his comings and goings. A-frames, being A-frames, don't allow for a lot of privacy, but we've managed to carve out enough to cohabitate without complaint. Housing on the Rez is notoriously hard to come by. The tribe owns the land, and the Fed holds it all in trust, so no real housing market exists, to speak of. If somebody wants to live on the Rez as a nonnative, they take whatever housing comes with the job.

The two of us have been awake from three or four onward for weeks now. At first, I didn't mind it. I made a very cogent and persuasive argument detailing how, in medieval times, the 3:00 a.m. hour was often used for sex. Caroline was on board. That was great for a while, but eventually, the novelty wore off. Now, she goes out to read while I usually lie as still as I can, hoping sleep will overtake me before I lose feeling in my sciatic-nerve area.

No such luck tonight. I get up and stretch to try to regain feeling in my outer ass and decide four thirty is as good a time as any to make sure I'm all prepped for the day.

I walk out to the den and find Caroline curled up under the gravity blanket—one of my few good infomercial buys from back in the day. She looks at me like I brought her out of a daydream.

"You all right?" I whisper, not wanting to wake Grant,

if, in fact, he's up there sleeping and not off trying to find some "personal space" with Kai, a feat that has become noticeably more difficult now that Hosteen is back in town.

"Sort of," she says, but she scoots over and makes room.

"Wanna talk about it?" I ask.

She watches the night sky outside of the square windows without really seeing it. I can always tell when her mind is in list mode. "It's the clinic, the Rez. All the raw smoke floating around, and…"

I take a seat and settle heavily into the couch. "And?"

"And now this Jacob Dark Sky you saw at the Bodreys'," she says after a moment. "It's all got the same strange feel to it. Of the other side."

She's avoiding my eyes, which is one of her tells. My guess is she had something else on her mind, something that went unsaid, but I know when not to pry. Learning this took me the better part of a decade, but I know.

"Not much we can do about Dark Sky. Just hope his 'cure' doesn't set Kai back too much and step in when he steps out. As for the clinic, let's see what's on deck for today."

I grab my box of a laptop and fire it up. Our Wi-Fi streams about as well as molasses, but I eventually get behind the VPN and into the health system. A quick glance at my schedule shows a strangely light patient load, but that doesn't mean much. We've had far more drop-ins than appointments over the past couple of weeks.

"The young Yageezi girl came back anemic, likely from heavy cycles. Same with the Two Leaf women. The Shiprock kids are harder to figure. Blood work came

back in range, but they were exhibiting signs of malnu-
trition. I think the lethargy might be iron-deficiency
related. Signs of pre-diabetes and full-blown type two
everywhere."

I flip through lab after lab until the words become a
blur, trying to pinpoint what's really bothering me. A few
crows cross the windowpane, and I try not to read into
that.

"None of it adds up," Caroline says, watching through
the window as the weak light of morning gathers over the
desert. The A-frame is in an old part of the Rez, put in
well before the IHS apartments to the south, but what this
neighborhood lacks in paved roads, it makes up for in
open vista.

"No. It doesn't add up to the crush we've seen. Particularly from the Arroyo squad." I rub my face, hoping to
clear my mind. I have a mountain of medical experience
on my back. I should be able to figure out why we're
getting hammered at the clinic. "I can treat what I see.
Play Whac-A-Mole. But on the whole, I don't know what's
going on here."

I say it quietly, as if my dad might somehow be
listening from beyond the grave.

Caroline pulls the blanket up around herself. "If this
place was a body, I'd say its immune system was getting
worn down. Stripped away. Remember you always used to
say 'soothe the symptom...'"

"But treat the cause." That's the age-old mantra of
Bennet medicine men. And until now, I've always been
able to do just that.

I'll be the first to admit that, more often than not, I'm
out of my depth as a father to Grant and a partner to
Caroline. But when I put on that white coat and step into

an exam room, I'm supposed to be the one in his element. The one others lean on, the one that delivers.

I slowly shut my laptop and stand. My back reminds me that I'm supposed to be asleep right now. Caroline folds the blanket up and carefully sets it aside, watching the crows gather silently in the dirt lot across the road. The sun still hasn't peeked over the horizon, but I don't need to see smoke to know that Caroline is thinking the same thing as I am.

Time to put on the coffee. We're going to need it.

CAROLINE and I are jacked on caffeine and expecting a crush when we walk through the CHC doors, but all we get is a trickle.

Of my nineteen appointment slots, three show up. The drop-ins are almost nonexistent. Up front, Dee looks just as spooked as she did when we were slammed and Caroline saw the smoke everywhere, but today, it's for a different reason. The silence is almost more unnerving than the noise.

Believe it or not, we have had a few calm days at the CHC in the past. Days when the patient load was light and the drop-ins just didn't come, days when we felt like the people within our sphere of influence, in general, were well.

This is not like one of those days.

The waiting room has an abandoned feel, the type of emptiness that makes me think we've hit some sort of glitch in the routine. Like we're one click to the left of the rest of the world. It's unsettlingly like the hollow feel of the thin place.

"Where is everybody?" I ask, half expecting my voice to echo.

Dee clacks away at her computer. "Looks like the cancellations started coming in late last night."

Caroline walks around the waiting room, straightening the chairs and tossing some stray water cups. She catches my glance, and I pop an eye that asks what her smoke sight says. She shakes her head minutely. If any smoke is still here, it's telling her nothing. She makes a full circle and peers out the door, furrowing her brow.

Dee tells me my late afternoon schedule is clear, which is something I'd have killed for a month ago but now strikes me as ominous. Dr. Sadler's schedule is the same. "Maybe we just pack it in," she says, rapping a tattoo on the faded countertop with her long nails.

Caroline walks outside.

"Hold that thought, Dee," I say. "We'll be right back."

Outside, Caroline is heading across the street to the Smoker's pop-up shop on the broken strip of sidewalk outside of the Quik-N-Go. He's been ripping people off with his "natural cures" there for so long that he's become as much of a fixture as the gas station. Looks like he's breaking things down, packing his junk away layer by layer in a blocky hiker's backpack. He looks up as Caroline approaches. The buzzing halogens overhead give him a sickly tint.

"Back again, paleface?" he asks her, not unkindly. "I knew I'd get you one day." He squints over at me. "And with a referral, too, I see."

"Where is everybody?" Caroline asks.

The Smoker takes in a deep breath and coughs daintily into a fist. He brushes his card table off. "Yesterday was a tough day at the office. Didn't even sell enough to buy a decent stick of tobacco. Today is looking much the same. Figure I'd cut my losses."

He looks longingly at the Quik-N-Go. The silence gets awkward.

The Smoker clears his throat again, and it sounds ugly. "I feel like cigarettes should be free for my people. Don't you? We basically taught your people what tobacco is. That should come with a lifetime pass for cigarettes."

I shoot a lost look toward Caroline.

She rolls her eyes. "He wants us to buy him cigarettes."

The Smoker puts his hands in the pockets of his jeans and looks innocently off into the distance. Caroline looks at me questioningly.

"Wait, you want me to go buy him a pack of cigarettes?"

Caroline shrugs. "He knows something." She turns toward the Smoker. "You know something, don't you?"

The smoker blinks placidly.

"I'm pretty sure that's some sort of violation of my Hippocratic oath," I say.

She shrugs. "The Quik-N-Go only takes cash. You're the one that carries cash."

The Smoker pops an eyebrow my way.

"Not a *lot* of cash," Caroline adds quickly. "Like, just a very little bit of cash. Look, I'll do it if you want."

"No, hold on," I mutter, digging out my wallet as I walk to the scratched-up window. The kid behind it looks about fourteen and stoned out of his mind. A ton of cigarettes sit on the shelves behind him. The Quik-N-Go basically sells cigarettes and energy drinks.

"Can you tell me what that fellow with the card table back there likes to smoke?"

The kid grabs a packet of some brand I've never heard

of and rings it up. I pay him and walk back before I can think too hard about it. I can honestly say this is my first cigarette purchase. *Forty-two-year streak broken right there.*

I slide it across the card table, and the Smoker gives me a little bow of thanks before slitting it open, flicking one out, and lighting up in what seems like one fluid motion. He takes a deep drag and nods toward the sky. Then another. I fight the urge to start asking questions, starting with the empty clinic across the street. I've learned the blunt approach doesn't work so well around here.

The Smoker holds the cigarette up to his line of sight like he's appraising the thing. "Switched to lights to go a bit easier on the ol' lungs," he says. "Sort of a New Year's resolution thing."

I tap my fingers together and clear my throat. Caroline gives me a tiny shake of the head, and I swallow what likely was going to be an unkind remark about the health merits of light cigarettes versus regular old cigarettes when one smokes forty a day. In short, you're dead either way. But if I went around offering unsolicited medical advice to every Navajo I saw, we'd be run out of town pretty quickly.

"Do you hear that?" he asks, eyes distant.

I listen but can't hear anything above the buzz of the halogen lights and the constant thwacking of the moths that flock to them in the summer. Not at first.

Then I catch a sound. Underneath it all is a distant keening, a soft cry that almost seems a part of the sky itself.

"That is Tsoodził talking. You call it Mount Taylor."

"Mount Taylor? No way. That's halfway to Albuquerque."

"When Tsoodził wants to be heard, distance doesn't matter."

Caroline shivers despite the heat. "So that's wind?"

Smoke rolls lazily from the Smoker's nose as he speaks. "Could be. Tsoodził talks when the wind blows. But Tsoodził also talks when the wind is going to blow."

He takes one last drag, all the way down to the filter. "Nobody showed up today, right? At the clinic?" He gently puts the cigarette out on the ground before stashing the butt in a pocket. "Back when I was selling... other things... at the Arroyo, if we saw a dip in business, we knew it was because another shop had moved in."

I blinked. "Now, hold on. What you do and what I do aren't really on the same—"

Caroline cuts me off. "Who moved in?"

The Smoker plucks a stray bit of ash from the sleeve of his threadbare Cleveland Indians baseball jersey and furrows his brow as he watches it float away on an indiscernible breeze. "Jacob Dark Sky."

The old Navajo's sightless gaze comes back to me in a flash. Same with the way that black bear totem blazed when he touched it. I swear he could almost see me while I phased.

"I thought he was just here for Kai," I say, my mouth dry. "Some nonsense to stop hand trembling, which in her case is simply a very treatable presentation of high blood sugar."

The Smoker ignores my digression, and I feel a bit like an idiot having blurted it out.

"Word got out that he was doing old medicine. Powerful medicine," he says, watching a stray bit of trash flip end over end through the empty CHC parking lot.

"People say he is strong in the old ways, stronger than the elder twins, even."

"What do you say?" Caroline asks.

His gaze turns toward her, and he seems taken aback for a moment. Shocked that anyone would care what he thinks, least of all one of us. But that's where Caroline gets people. Not only does she ask, she actually cares. It's in her DNA.

"I don't know what to think," he says. "But I know Dark Sky is starting a Holyway tonight. Rumor is it's some kind of Windway. And I'm invited."

The Smoker shrugs on his loaded pack. Settles it carefully on his back. "A true Windway takes days. But I hear Dark Sky is on another level."

"And you really believe all this?" I ask, trying and failing to keep my cynical half at bay.

The Smoker clears a wheezy rumble in his chest and scratches gingerly at that spot on his neck again.

"He'd better be," he says. "Otherwise I think I'm in real trouble."

The Smoker walks off down the sidewalk without another word. That strange wind picks up a notch, the one he says rips around Mount Taylor even though it's too far away even to catch a glimpse of on a clear day.

I believe that the Smoker and I are on opposite ends of pretty much everything, and I think he'd be the first to agree. But on this, he and I see eye to eye.

It feels like we're all walking into trouble.

6

CAROLINE ADAMS

Whenever Grant has a problem and he doesn't know what to do about it, he does this thing where he awkwardly takes up space in your general vicinity because he doesn't really know how to start the conversation he wants to have. Just sort of hangs around, hands in the pockets of his jeans and a preoccupied look on his face.

I think it's something ingrained from the days when he was a kid, not even ten years old but already on his own a lot. His grandfather loved him, but Abernathy was old school and distant. He had to figure out a lot of adult stuff by himself, at an age when kids shouldn't be worrying about much of anything.

Grant told me once that when he was young, a group of older middle school kids chased him on his bike for three straight years every day after school. Kids, being kids, don't really care if you're an orphan or not. Middle school kids can be especially monstrous. But he dealt with it—mostly by running, which I totally get.

That kind of a childhood turns boys into men who have difficulty asking for help.

The third time I turn around in our little box of a kitchen and nearly bump into him, I say, "Alright, out with it."

"What?" Grant asks, suddenly picking at his thumbnail.

"Usually, you're always out doing something, here, there, in the garage, anywhere. When you stand around like this, something's up. It's Kai, isn't it?"

Grant is still somehow surprised that I guessed right. I'm not sure what exactly he thinks I do all day when he's on those twenty-minute phone calls with her, walking around the A-frame like it's a running track. That Texas twang carries for days out here.

"I gave her the pump and the monitor and told her Dad would teach her how to configure the whole thing, but..."

"But what?"

Grant scratches at the surprisingly well-filled-in scruff at his chin. *When did that get there?* Every time I stand next to him, he seems taller. And a little more unsure. Especially when I remember the little eight-year-old boy he was, marching fearlessly into the Arroyo for the first time with a bird on his head. The longer we live, the more of that raw confidence seems to go out the window.

"But something ain't right. Hos took her back to the trading post, where he's putting up with that guy Dad saw, some medicine man from the Colorado Creek reservation out west named Jacob Dark Sky. But the elder twins don't know him, and Chaco says he ain't how he seems..."

I put my hands on his arms and try to will his smoke calmer. It's changed color over the years. I remember when he was a boy, it bopped around him like a puppy, the harvest-brown color of goose down. It's darker now, stronger, searching. It still calms at my touch. I bank that one. *Still got it.* I'll try to remember that when I feel like I'm dropping every other ball in my life.

"Where's Chaco?" I ask.

That bird is our first line of defense in the spiritual world but also in the world of Grant's mind. And now that I think about it, I haven't heard the rustle of his wings in a while.

"He was with me at the Arroyo. But he went across to the other side of the veil. He's been over there more and more."

Grant leaves it at that, but I know what he means. Chaco has been looking for Ben. With very little success.

"Is everything okay over there?" I ask, trying to keep my voice as professional as possible, which I realize is an odd thing to do when talking to family.

Grant runs a hand through his hair, longer now than it's ever been. "He says a bad wind is rising in the thin place. That it's been gathering bit by bit for a while now. How, or why, he can't say. Just that it's been a long time coming, and Dark Sky showing up made it a lot worse."

When I first met Grant, he and Owen and I fought our way through a mess that came through a break in the thin place in the black desert of West Texas. Let's just say it was not a super fun time. The longer we've lived here in relative peace, the more that whole ordeal feels like it happened to someone else. Like they told me about it over some very strong cocktails.

But it didn't. It happened to me. To us. And now, something is happening again.

"I feel it too," I say. "It's like the smoke is... looking that way. Toward the Bodrey place."

"I wish I knew what Dark Sky is gonna do to her," he says, his eyes pleading.

"Do you want me to go out there?" I ask. In a way, I'm flattered. Grant thinks I might actually be able to hold my own with a bunch of radical bootleggers and a self-professed Navajo holy man in the Rez backcountry. That's just nuts. Right now, I'm having difficulty deciding if I can finish the mac-n-cheese I set out to make in this kitchen.

"Just a quick phase in and out. I want to know what I'm up against, and I thought since you can see things, maybe you'll see something Dad missed."

I can't help but think how Owen would be hurt to hear Grant talk like this. He would never let it show, of course. At least not until it came spilling out of him at three in the morning, when both of us are staring at the ceiling above the bed.

Owen *has* been pulling double shifts at the CHC. He's staying late right now, manning the after-hours clinic, hoping someone shows up. That's part of who he is, and I love him for it, but it's the type of drive that sometimes lends itself to a sort of "male refrigerator blindness" when it comes to noticing things. And he can't see the smoke like I can.

Plus, Grant's right. I can be in and out.

Fine. Just a peek.

TWO STEPS in the thin place takes me to the doorstep of the Bodrey trading post. I'm there in seconds. I bet the pot of water I left simmering for the mac still has another five minutes until it's boiling. Yes, I realize that is unsafe, but Grant is there. The other week, I phased to meet Owen at a house call in Sheep Springs, and when I phased back to the A-frame, I realized I'd left the sink running for, like, twenty minutes.

Half of me is trying to avoid thinking of the phrase *baby brain.* The other half can't help but wonder if phasing is good for a tiny ball of cells in my uterus. If said tiny ball of cells exists, that is. I still get stage fright every time I look at that pregnancy test. That's all it takes to get the anxiety ball rolling in my head.

Thankfully, Jacob Dark Sky is here to distract me.

He's standing on the packed dirt in front of the warped wooden front steps of the trading post, along with Hosteen, as if expecting me. He's old but not diminished, even shirtless, which is saying something. The high-summer insects pepper the hissing propane lights, but they don't bother him. A cane is propped against one knee as though it's an accessory. In the streaming sepia of the in-between place, his eyes are completely black, and I know in an instant that he's blind. He's exactly as Owen described.

What Owen can't have seen is the pure white smoke that streams from Dark Sky's eyes, wafting with the movement of his head as he speaks to Hosteen, settling over the two of them and most of the porch like a halo of smoke.

The scene is so shocking that I need a moment to register that he's paused in whatever discussion I stepped in on.

Dark Sky tilts his head like a dog trying to pick up a sound.

"What is it?" Hosteen asks, looking around and through me.

Dark Sky can't see me either—that's the rule of this place—but he's not totally missing me like Hosteen. He may be blind to the physical world, but he's picking something up in the place between. The white smoke pouring from his eyes spreads out around him like probing roots. One weaves its way toward me with creepy intention.

"Nothing," says Dark Sky, thumbing the banded silver grip of his cane. "Just a whisper on the wind is all. Perhaps a visitor. But this will be a ceremony that calls visitors."

The probing smoke scatters in the wind. Hosteen says something in Navajo that I can't follow as Dark Sky slowly stands and grabs a pinch of pollen from a worn leather satchel at his waist.

"We are announcing ourselves, Hosteen. What comes will come. And is welcome." He dusts the pollen over Hosteen's head and hands the pouch over. Hosteen does the same to Dark Sky.

"Come," Dark Sky says. "The hogan is ready."

Hosteen looks at him strangely. "Why are you speaking in English?"

Dark Sky looks out over the valley below the trading post, where a hogan made of brush is glowing like a paper lantern in the dark sea of sand.

"Come," he says again, planting his cane firmly. "It takes me longer to walk downhill these days than I'd like to admit, and we need to get started."

Hosteen follows, his question unanswered and likely forgotten. But I know why Dark Sky spoke English.

He was talking to me.

I gauge the distance between where I stand and the glowing hogan below. Far for an old blind man, maybe, but not for me. I take a practiced stutter step and zip on down.

I'm on the flat below even as Dark Sky and Hosteen are still bobbing shapes against the red-rock face of the cliff above. They're making their slow way from the top of Crooked Snake down a path that looks like it was carved by the persistent press of millions of footfalls.

I take a deep breath. A lot about the crow totem scares the crap out of me, but I'm a big fan of the half-mile shuffle. I was never very fast as a kid, and running still makes my legs itch. But with my crow, I can beat darn near everybody on this living plane anywhere.

The hogan in front of me is unlike any I've seen before. Traditional hogans—the ones just off the Arroyo —are made of clay and mud and framed out to a dome shape with a door facing east, toward the rising sun. They're functional but not exactly charming, unless you really love sitting on dirt—pretty claustrophobic too. But I think that's the point. It's a bit like a kiln. Add some heat and smoke, the right ceremonies and people, and those who enter can come out changed.

But those are the Arroyo hogans. This one reminds me a little bit of a wedding canopy. I know if Grant could hear my thoughts, he'd roll his eyes until they were in danger of dropping out, and the Smoker would say, "Prime white-people shit." But hey, I call it like I see it. And what I see are four big pine logs, their wood rubbed so smooth that they shine in the evening sun, holding up a canopy of woven piñon branches.

It's very pretty. The whole scene here on the flat would be wedding-planner worthy if not for Kai, glassy eyed and partially slumped next to a central fire pit underneath those freshly cut piñon branches.

The sight of her like this hits me harder than I would've expected. I let go of my crow and flash through into reality before I even know what I'm doing. I'm at her side in an instant, checking her pulse, feeling her brow, and trying to get her to track my finger. I'm in full Nurse Mode before it occurs to me that Dark Sky and Hosteen are minutes from discovering me here.

Kai is in a thin leather getup that looks ceremonial. She leans on me without really meaning to. "Mom?" she asks, disoriented and lost. "I feel weird."

Her cinnamon skin is ashy and her forehead drenched in sweat. Her tongue sticks to the roof of her mouth when she talks. She blinks and rubs at her eyes, trying to focus. *Blurry vision. Cotton mouth. Could be ketotic hyperglycemia.* Owen and I have seen far too much of it go untreated around here. Her blood sugar is probably through the roof.

"Honey, you need to lie down," I say, and I look around helplessly as tears come to my eyes. I hear a distant chanting, Dark Sky singing his way in. He'll see me in seconds, if he hasn't already.

Kai lies down, presses her forehead to the cool dirt, and gets lost in the fire. She needs insulin. Maybe the pump Grant gave her is somewhere in the trading post, but even if I found it, I couldn't carry it through when phasing. What she really needs is a hospital bed and an endocrinologist. I take out my phone, thinking I can call the IHC emergency line. *No service, of course.* Sometimes, I wonder why the hell I even bother having a phone on this reservation.

The voices are very close now.

"Kai?" It's Hosteen, his voice hard, sensing something is wrong.

"I'll be right here," I whisper to her. That's all I can say, all I can do.

I grab the crow the second I see the toe of Hosteen's boot poke around the branches. Kai and the summer hogan become a sand-colored wash, blurred at the edges. The bite of the thin place is instant, but I've gotten better at withstanding it. The longer I can stick it out, the better chance I've got at figuring out how to help Kai.

Hosteen sees his sister and rushes over to her. Kneeling down, he places one hand gently on her shoulder. True worry fills his eyes. I know because it's in his smoke too. It looks strange on him, like seeing a scarred pit bull nuzzle up to someone.

"Kai! What's wrong?" He looks helplessly over at Dark Sky. "What's happened to her?"

Dark Sky scans the space where I stand, the white smoke seeps forth, and I get an odd two-faced sensation of a man that looks both hard and determined and also like strange tears are streaming down his face.

His smoke shifts to Kai, and he hitches up his cane to kneel next to her. The white from his eyes envelops her like fog rolling over a flat lake.

"Have strength," he says. "It will get worse before it gets better. That is the way with ghost sickness."

Hosteen removes his hand from his sister, his face pained. He starts praying under his breath in Navajo, soft and rhythmic. Dark Sky pulls something from his pouch and tosses it into the fire, herbs and something else that looks like a black totem, but before I can get a good look, it's instantly consumed, and in that same moment, I feel a wind.

I blink.

I've never felt wind in the thin place before, only the bite of being too close to the veil. This place is a weird in-between. No sensations exist here except for that awful cold—until now.

This ghost wind rips right through the patchy frame of the summer hogan and stands the flame of the center fire pit up like a torch. But it doesn't touch anyone or anything else in the living plane. Not even a hair stirs on Kai's beaded forehead.

So this Dark Sky is more than he looks. That's fine. We can deal with this, I tell myself even as I'm nibbling at my thumbnail like it's covered in fine Swiss chocolate.

Dark Sky starts to sing. I understand none of it, only what I feel, and what I feel is that it's an old song, really old. The words sound Navajo, but they're like Navajo that's been dug up from the deep, as if each word is blown free of dirt as he speaks it.

I watch in horror as Dark Sky reaches directly into the fire with both hands and grabs two fistfuls of ash. He doesn't break at all in his singing, doesn't seem to notice the flame as he rubs the ash over his hands and then up and down his arms. What's left, he streaks across his blind eyes like a mask.

Sparks from the fire swirl around the hogan, the wind whips Kai's hair around her head, and she starts to seize. I step toward her on instinct and almost walk my way right out of the thin place. Only the force of the weird wind saves me. Reminds me where I am. I hold tight to the crow.

Dark Sky goes digging in the fire again with his black hands, longer than anyone should or could, until he pulls out the totem. When he presses it to his blind eyes, I see it's a bear, cut roughly from some sort of glittery black rock.

He pops the totem into his mouth and sings loudly.

The bear bobs along on his tongue, and the song never breaks. I feel sick. Whenever gross body things happened in nursing school, I would always blink rapidly, sort of like covering my eyes without covering my eyes. I'm doing it now, but if the totem hurts Dark Sky at all, he doesn't show it—no searing smoke, no burning flesh. Just a cold glitter.

Dark Sky turns toward Kai and grabs her by both arms. Hosteen picks up the chant where Dark Sky leaves off. He doesn't have nearly the force behind his voice, but he seems to know what he's doing. Dark Sky lays Kai down and straddles her. She doesn't really fight, which makes me sick all over again. He leans over her face and sucks at the totem and spits to one side. He does this again and again, like he's sucking some unseen poison from the air above her.

The rational part of me—the part that still has her nursing textbooks, highlighted in nine different colors, in a box under the bed—knows that a totem cannot be used to suck away a diabetic seizure. That's not how it works.

But when Kai's seizure calms, and her panting slows to a cadence of normal breathing, I have to set that part aside. I have to let weird Caroline step in, the one that knows calming smoke can help, if it's done right—at least until we can get the insulin.

Dark Sky spits again into the fire, which is close enough to Kai's head to make this double gross, then he nods. He takes a thumb and paints a whorl of ash on Kai's forehead, still damp with sweat. "It is done."

Hosteen nearly collapses as he rushes back to his sister's side. He reaches for her arm again but pauses.

"You may touch her," Dark Sky says. "She is clean. But there are a great many others who are not."

Hosteen does, softly squeezing her shoulder and speaking low in Navajo. This is about as brotherly as I've ever seen the guy—it's a shame Kai is basically unconscious for it.

When the wind dies down, the burn of the thin place comes back full force. A cold pinch works its way slowly into my skin like a large-gauge needle. Time to bounce.

"We have work to do, Hosteen." Those are the words I hear Dark Sky utter as I step away and the summer hogan is sucked back behind me.

One step. Two. Three. Then I'm back in the A-frame.

I let go of the crow, and my legs go all loose on me, and I sort of topple right into Grant's arms.

"Mom! What is it? Are you hurt?"

He helps me upright. He's so strong now, and wide. The thin little boy with the crow on his head is gone. It makes me a little sad.

"He's the real deal," I say, sucking in the sun-warmed pine smell of the A-frame like it's ice-cold water in the middle of a dry desert night. "Jacob Dark Sky. I don't know what kind of deal he is, but I know he's real. His power comes from the bell side of things," I say. "From the crow side. Ben's side. And it's growing."

Grant taps the bell absently, eyes tracing thoughts that I can see as ripples racing through his smoke. "What about Kai?" he asks.

"She seems okay. For now. Although how and why, I have no idea. She shouldn't be. He stopped a hypoglycemic seizure with a totem and a whorl of ash on her forehead. None of it makes any sense."

The front door opens, and Owen walks through. He's as put together as ever, his white coat crisp over a button-down and tie. But his eyes are tired, disheartened. My guess is the clinic never picked up.

He slows his steps as he comes in. I must not look too good either. Frazzled, pale, sucking wind. Grant still has a hand on my shoulder like he's old-lady escorting me across the street.

"What did I miss?" he asks slowly.

I don't even know where to begin. I feel the steam and the heat and the ghost wind of the summer hogan still, as if it's come back with me.

No, wait, that's just from the pot on the stove. The mac-n-cheese water is still boiling.

7

OWEN BENNET

I'm taking off my tie and rolling up my sleeves, and Grant is watching me with one shoulder leaned against the doorframe in that unnervingly calm way of his. After a moment, I bite, reiterating myself again. "Absolutely not, Grant. Your mother and I can get in and out. You can do no such thing."

Grant pops an eyebrow. He was always like this, clear-eyed even as a young boy, calm and collected in situations where his peers would likely have wet themselves. He's grown even more stoic over the past few years here. He reminds me more and more of the Navajo that way.

"Really?" he asks flatly. "I'm the whole reason any of you are doing this at all. She's my girlfriend. I need to see this through."

Caroline is in the living room, fortified with mac-n-cheese, pulling her hair back into what she calls her "phase pony," and it's impossibly attractive, which isn't what I really need right now, preparing to go into the breach as we are. What's needed is calm focus so that we can make the right decisions, just like in surgery. I need to be a lot like, well, a lot like Grant, honestly.

Caroline checks herself in the mirror. Tightens the ponytail. Loosens the ponytail. "Honey, it's not like that. We're just trying to understand what this Dark Sky guy is doing here. Once we get a game plan, we'll tackle it together. Nobody is leaving you out."

Grant gives her a flat look, crossing his arms. "I think that's kind of the definition of what you're doing. By going without me."

I can hear Chaco's massive talons skittering across the roof, and I'm surprised at how relieved I feel. It's been a while since I've seen him. I think Chaco will take our side. He knows better than anyone that the bell must be kept safe.

"So let me get this straight, Mom," Grant says, as if reading off a dinner menu. "You tell me Dark Sky pinned her down and did some sort of exorcism while she was having a seizure, and I'm *not* supposed to go check on her?"

Caroline soaks the mac-n-cheese pot and purses her lips. I can tell that sounds as ridiculous to her as it does to me. The bottom line is the Bodrey place has never been safe, even before Dark Sky came around. I don't want Grant anywhere near it. I don't want the bell there either, but mostly, I don't want Grant there, not until we can gather the Circle and figure out what's happening.

Telling Grant to hold back is hard. He's eighteen. He holds the key to the door between worlds around his neck. We come from different places. When I was eighteen, the high point of my year was when my father gave me a nod of approval at getting into medical school. I still remember that nod. Then Caroline came into my life, and then Grant came into my life, and my heart made room for him just like it did for her. *How am I supposed to tell him to stay away from his Caroline?*

Thankfully, *my* Caroline taps in. "All we're asking is for you to stay here while we figure out what's going on. Can you do that?" She looks at me.

Grant lets out a long, slow sigh, but he moves over to the couch and sits down.

"Alright," I say, checking my pants for my wallet and keys before realizing neither will get me very far where I'm going. "That's that, then. We'll be right back."

I open the door and step out, holding it for Caroline like we're just hopping over to Manuelito's for a Christmas-style enchilada. Grant watches us from the couch, his unblinking gaze skeptical. The night wind picks up again, and I have to shield my eyes from the fine desert silt sliding across the road out front. Up on the roof, Chaco pivots himself against it, low and sleek in the moonlight.

Tonight, I don't need to be linked to the bird to know what he's saying. Whatever is going on up Crooked Snake Road, it's like the wind is running ahead of us, pulling us there.

Chaco is telling me to watch my step.

8

GRANT ROMER

After I hear the soft *whoosh pop* that follows Mom and Dad's exit, I wait another ten seconds on the couch, then I get up and grab my keys. I can hear Chaco's exasperated sigh in my mind.

"Yeah, right," I say. "Like you ever thought for a second I wasn't goin' up there too."

Chaco's voice is a slow roll in my head. "They're just trying to keep you safe, man."

"I'm pretty good at lookin' out for myself. I'm not a—"

"Not a kid anymore. Yeah, yeah. Now you're old enough to make the *really* bad decisions. Congratulations."

I shrug on my beat-up trucker jacket and make sure the door's locked on the way out. "Somethin's coming. I can feel it. The bell can feel it."

"Something's already here," Chaco says, his eyes following me from the roof.

I hop in the truck and fire it up. The lights catch the desert sand whirling down the hardpack. If I go maybe a little faster than I should, I can get to the Bodrey place in under an hour, hopefully before things start heating up.

I pause, one hand on the gear shift. "Still can't find Ben?" I ask.

Chaco spreads his wings and floats erratically down to the ground. "Oh, I can find him. That's not the problem."

"Where is he, then? He's gotta know things ain't right here."

Chaco's voice is troubled. "It's hard to explain. I still don't really get it myself. But it's all connected to what's going on out back of the trading post."

I throw the truck into gear, and it rocks gently as a big gust skitters grit against the side facing the dark plains. "So does that mean you're coming?"

Chaco struts over to the truck and hops up to the open window. "Of course I'm coming. But I sure as hell ain't flying. Tricky winds these days. A couple bad gusts, and I might end up blown halfway to Mexico."

He unceremoniously flops his way over my lap, buffeting me with his wings until he's sitting shotgun. "Come to think of it, Mexico sounds pretty nice right about now."

I pick a stray bit of black fluff from the scruff of my jawline and let it fly out the window on the wind. "Why go to Mexico when you can go to the Bodrey trading post?"

Chaco laughs, a funny tittering sound I've always loved. Another gust broadsides the truck with sand, but the engine roars back as we take off, side by side, into some sort of trouble.

Just like old times.

~

Turns out I don't need to worry about anyone spotting my truck on Crooked Snake. I can't get much more than halfway up the pass. Beat-up trucks and rusted-out cars are parked end to end wherever the shoulder gives them room. I recognize a lot of them from the Arroyo.

"I think we're better off parking near the turnoff," Chaco says warily. "Last one in, first one out, and all that."

I skid to a stop and throw my truck into reverse. "All this is for Dark Sky?"

Chaco chirrups an affirmative.

"Who is this guy, some kind of rock star?"

Chaco's stony gaze follows the broken line of darkened cars as we pass, his head making little tics. "I'm getting more of a tent-revival vibe."

When I shut the lights off, the darkness is complete. The wind isn't gusting anymore, but I can still hear it somehow, a soft, consistent keening like a coyote gearing up to howl.

I get out, walk around, and pop open Chaco's door.

He hops up to perch on the top of the door frame, where he's eye to eye with me. "I'm gonna scout ahead a bit while the wind is down. Fly low. See what I can see."

"Guess I'll start walking."

Chaco puts one claw on my shoulder. "Watch out for snakes. It's called Crooked Snake Road for a reason."

Chaco and I are about as close as can be, but he's never been the touchy-feely sort, so whenever he does something like this, it kind of gets to me, in a good way. I run my thumb over the dome of his head, flush with the downy feathers of his brow. He leans into it a bit, and I realize he's worried, really worried, about me but also about this whole production.

That, and he knows I really don't like snakes.

I tap the heel of my trusty boots against the steel runner of the truck. "I'll be all right. I got my stompers on."

Chaco looks unimpressed. Then again, I ain't ever really seen any bird look impressed. He stretches his wings and takes off into the night, ten feet up in a span of wingbeats, then gone to my eye but not my mind.

I grab my hat and start walking.

The pass really is as crooked as it sounds. A series of switchbacks cuts through the red rock. At times, the road looks like it could take two cars. Other times, it looks more like those bottlenecks that shepherds squeeze their flocks through. I know a handful are out here. Strange to think of peaceful little sheep milling around bootleg country and munching Saragossa grass feet from pressurized stills that could blow at any minute.

I'm about a half mile in when I hear the first snake. The rattle sounds like bones in a bean can. Before I can call out, Chaco says, "Stay cool. Stick to the middle of the road. They don't want anything to do with you."

His voice knocks my heartbeat down a level or two until I find the words. "What do you mean *they*?"

Chaco drops down low and buzzes me, his version of *I got you, bro*. Then he's up again, out and above in a few wingbeats. I remember to breathe.

"Let's just say there are, uh, quite a few snakes," Chaco says.

Now that he's told me, I can hear them. They scratch the bushes and shift the dirt with a sound that's a bit like rolling up a garden hose.

"The good news is they don't seem to care about you," Chaco says, passing back and over again.

I feel a snake brush past the outer edge of my right

boot and only manage to clip a scream by biting my tongue. Another slides by on my left.

"We're all headed to the same place," Chaco says. "It's like they can't even see you. Just keep your head."

I try not to pick up my feet, moving through the dirt at a light shuffle for another five minutes until I can see the Bodrey trading post through a cut in the canyon. The building itself is dark and shuttered, but a torch blazes on the lip of the ridge just beyond. I've been up here a few times, and I know that torch marks the start of the canyon steps that take you to the Bodrey back-country.

I dash to the first marker and take a minute to catch my breath. The ringing in my ears is slowly replaced by another sound, rhythmic and swaggering—a chant. The singer's voice carries even all the way up here.

"Looks like we're late to the party," Chaco says.

The glittering scene on the flat below sucks the wind from me all over again. A big summer hogan glows like a lantern, open at the sides. A campfire inside seems to dance in time with the chant. I count roughly a hundred people spread out around it. A crown of smaller pit fires rings this crowd, their smoke feeding the black of the sky. Beyond that, the dark moves, flashing every now and then with the dull glint of snakeskin.

The bell warms in warning on my chest. Best not to look too hard into that darkness.

"What the hell kind of Diné ceremony would call on snakes? The Diné and I have the same views on snakes. Not huge fans."

I can feel Chaco's mind working like the whirring of a clock. He can tap into memories and experiences so vast and deep that if he let me in on 'em, I'd probably go crazy.

Before he was with me, he was with Ben's grandma. Safe to say he knows a thing or two about Diné ceremonies.

"A Windway shows the power of Great Snake," Chaco says. "But it's in the song and the sandpainting. Not slithering through the darkness."

I stick close to the shadowy side of the cliff face as I walk toward the next pit fire. They're made from cans of lard, but they smell sweet, like sage, and underneath is a waft of manure every now and then.

"What kind of power?" I ask.

"To call forth lightning and thunder against those who have left the Navajo Way. To cleanse them."

At the second marker, the path switches back again and cuts deeper against the hill. The chant provides its own beat, or maybe the crowd provides it for the Singer. Whatever it is, the sound is strangely hypnotic, like it wants to pull me toward it.

"I get the feelin' we may be in for some rough weather, then—"

"Get against the dirt," Chaco snaps.

I press flat at a spot where the wash and wind has cut the path to form a lip right over my head. I just manage to flatten against the canyon wall as snakes slide down the rock face, falling gracelessly through the air a foot from my head and landing on the path with heavy thunks like baseballs plunking the dirt one after the other. I'm too terrified to swallow, let alone move.

"You alright?" Chaco asks, his voice pitched with nerves.

"Hell no, I ain't alright."

Chaco's voice is strained. "She's front and center, chief, right up by the fire. Can you see her?"

I do. Kai stands against the backdrop of the whirling

sparks, swaying in time with the chant, fingers spread in a controlled trembling as she sweeps her arm back and forth over the crowd. The firelight plays on her bare shoulders.

For a moment, she is all I can see. She tilts her head back and bares her throat to the sky, eyes closed and lips open. I can taste the sweat on her throat from a hundred yards.

Jacob Dark Sky is behind the flame, deep within the summer hogan. His voice rings with the strength of a megaphone. He's dressed down to a breechcloth, and his body glistens. His long white braid is dripping wet. A fine string of black sand sluices from his cupped hand onto a cleared section of hardpack.

He pauses in his sandpainting and looks up, and for a moment, I swear his blind eyes sweep over me. The bell warms in warning again. High above, Chaco wheels in a slow circle.

"This guy *is* blind, right?" I ask.

Chaco titters. "That's the rumor. Either way, I'd stick close to that dirt."

Now that I'm here, I wonder how on earth I ever thought I could get Kai clear of this. She's in deep. I'd expected to find her scared, maybe even held hostage. Instead, she's walking through the crowd with one arm out like a dowsing rod. When she opens her eyes again, they burn with crazy. Her hand trembles as Dark Sky's song hits a high pitch. She's found a young girl, sitting on the ground, rocking, arms wrapped around her knees. When she lays the hand on the girl's shoulder, she stills, looks up, then eventually nods. Their way back to the fire is open.

Dark Sky stands in front of the flames to take them,

looking nothin' like the old man I'd been expecting. Blind or not, this guy is a shit kicker. He takes the girl behind the fire, and I lose sight of her. If this really is a Windway, that'll be the spot for the unraveling, where the fetishes are spun out from their sinew wrappings.

The whole scene is so surreal and the look in Kai's eye so weird that I forget all about the snakes until one plops right on my shoulder.

I try to scream, but a hand clamps over my mouth. Not a snake but an arm. A big arm.

"What the hell are you doing here, Keeper?" Joey hisses. "Are you out of your mind?"

Truth be told, I'm beginning to think I should've listened to Mom and Dad, but I'm not about to admit that to Joey.

Chaco dips low and lands on the lip in a cloud of dust, clicking his tongue in that way that says, *No shit.* "Told you, chief," he says. "We coulda been in Mexico."

"But Kai's in trouble, and—"

"And you thought you could come in here and white knight her out," Joey finishes, shaking his head.

"I know I wasn't invited."

"I do not care if you were invited or not. What I care about is you. As soon as you showed up, the crows started burning. Every Circle member knows you're here. And if they know, whatever *he* is probably does too." Joey nods toward Dark Sky.

Somehow, my parents knowing I'm here turns my gut about as much as the possibility of Dark Sky knowing. "So Mom and Dad..."

"Oh yeah. They are *not* happy. I sent them out to take a breather, manage the burn, while I talked to you first." By that, he means he did me a solid—again.

"Thanks, Joey."

Joey says nothing but maybe nods a millimeter.

We watch together in silence for a minute.

"Must be hard to see her like this," he says.

"I don't even know what *this* is," I say.

"Nobody seems to know. The Circle had no answers."

In the depths of the hogan, framed in flame, Dark Sky pins the arms of the new girl to the dirt by the sand-painting and brings his face close to hers.

"He's got some sort of totem in his mouth he uses for sucking poison," Joey says. "The sandpainting shows wind, lightning, snakes, but I've never seen a Windway quite like this, with this many sick. That's the fifth Arroyo kid Kai has brought back to Dark Sky."

"All Arroyo?"

Joey's keen gaze never wavers as he watches the summer hogan. "Everyone here is Arroyo," he says.

Chaco croaks low at that news. His beady eyes glitter with reflected flame. I try to catch his meaning, but he's turned away, lost in thoughts that are kept from me.

After a moment, Dark Sky pulls the girl to standing. She weaves, woozy, and the others steady her while Dark Sky holds the totem toward the sky.

"It's a black bear," Joey says. "He wraps it up in sinew and then starts all over again. Unraveling, offering prayer sticks to the four corners, a sweat. He's been at it for hours."

The bell thrums in time with the song. I grab it over my shirt without even realizing it, pull softly against it like it's a too-tight collar, and when I look back up, Kai's looking directly at me.

The sweat on the back of my neck chills in an instant.

"Stay still," Joey mutters. "We're not in trouble unless she decides she wants to make a thing out of it."

Kai's face is intense, jaw set, but her eyes tell a different story, like she's helpless, being pulled along. She slowly splays her fingers in my direction. After a moment, her hand trembles.

"Okay, now we're in trouble," Joey says.

That's all it takes for Mom and Dad to pop into existence right next to me.

Mom's already midlecture, like she started reading me the riot act back in the thin place. Her whisper is furious. "Grant Romer, we asked you to do one thing—one simple thing. Stay home!"

Dad's revved up too, which is saying something. "Son, is it so hard for you to believe that we might be doing what's best for you, what's best for the bell?"

Mom turns toward Chaco. "And don't even get me started with you. Isn't this your whole job?"

But Chaco is watching me carefully. He knows why I had to come. He gets me better than anybody in the whole world.

"I gotta go to her," I say.

Dad blinks a mile a minute. "Absolutely out of the question."

"You can't see her like we can, Grant," Mom says. "Her smoke is not right. Dark Sky did something to her. Changed her. I don't know what he is, but I do know he's dangerous."

Joey's eyes narrow as he nods in agreement. "Dark Sky is a stranger to the Dinétah, the land between the four sacred mountains."

"I thought you said he was Navajo," Dad whispers.

"He is. But he's also something else. And that makes him more dangerous. He's like…"

I get what Joey's thinking: Dark Sky is a Diné with one foot in the real world and one outside of it. He's a bit like Ben, but in a bad way.

Chaco reads my thoughts. "And Ben is the only one that can stop him," says the bird, with quiet power that settles my jumpy brain.

I know what I have to do even if I'm not sure why I have to do it yet. But knowing and doing are two different things, and the longer I wait, the harder this gets. Especially since now Hos sees me. His hungry smile is the kind of thing that used to wake me up screaming as a little kid back in Midland and send me to that little space between the dresser and the wall where I would get as small as I could and hope whatever brushed at my brain just kept on going. I didn't know Hos then, but I knew that smile.

I can hear my mother muttering to herself, "Where the hell is Ben?" as if it might call him this way.

"I'm afraid the Walker has forgotten this place," Joey says, his voice low and slow, like he's just now coming to terms with what he's saying. Joey holds on hard to Ben even though it's been years. After my parents died, I stared out the window every night, expecting their car to roll up even though the logical part of my brain knew damn well that car was totaled and my parents with it. The mind is a funny thing, though. I still stared out that window for months.

Chaco steps carefully onto my shoulder and settles himself. "You have to go with Hos," he says, mind to mind.

"I know. But why?"

He bumps the crown of his head softly against my ear. "For the Walker. So he'll hear."

Hosteen and another of his crew are close now, clearing the ground in big, sure steps.

"Will he come back?"

"I don't know. All I know is this story has played out before. In the Dinétah, everything comes around again."

This is what's been going on in his cosmic bird brain. This is what he's been staring at in the distance. I might only have half an idea of what he's talking about, but his word is good enough for me. Looks like things need to be kicked into motion, and I'm the one supposed to do the kickin'.

But one thing I am sure of. I ain't waiting for Hos to get me. I meet him on my own terms—just like I have for years.

As I step forward, Dad stops me with a hand to my free shoulder. "Don't do this."

He's not ordering. He's just asking. The fear that sits just below his words almost stops me, almost turns me right into him, to the crook of his arm, where I put myself when I soaked in his blood that one terrible day on the streets of Santa Fe, before he willed himself alive again.

My dad is a strong man, but he can't help us here. Only I can. And he sees the answer in my eyes.

"He'll take the bell," he says, his whisper harsh.

"I know."

"Then why?" Mom asks, stepping in close.

All I can say is what Chaco told me, what I feel. "To shake some things loose before Dark Sky takes everything."

That's all Joey needs to hear. He steps aside, clearing the path before me.

Hos emerges from the darkness, glowing in the fire-light. His eyes gleam. "And here you are," he says, twitchy, a bit like he's talking to himself. "Right where Dark Sky said you'd be."

Mom moves right into his face and sizes him up like a piece of meat. She leans back my way. "His smoke says he's not going to hurt you."

Hos furrows his brow, confused. I realize that maybe he isn't entirely in control of this situation either, which makes all of us.

"You sure about that?" Dad mutters.

"Pretty sure," Mom says.

Dad clears his throat. "*Pretty* sure?"

Chaco chimes in. "You gotta go, either way, chief."

I cut the back-and-forth short by just walking away from them, past Joey, past Hos. I don't even stop walking when he catches up and grabs my arm in a way that makes me doubt Mom's smoke read for a second.

"Easy, Hos. I ain't runnin'."

"Maybe you should," he hisses.

I never take my eyes off Kai, not even when I can feel the heat from the fire. I've been scrambling for days to get here, and now here she is. She's the same girl I've known for years, with the same black-lacquer hair, long and smooth, the same gorgeous skin, softly textured by the fire in the night. The difference is the thousand-yard stare. She's lost, wandering around somewhere inside her own head, trying to piece things together.

I take hold of her trembling hand in both of mine, but she pulls it gently away. "You should never have come," she says. "I have to go with Dark Sky."

I reach out for her again—no luck. "Go where?" I ask.

Hos pulls me back, and I shove his hand away, which pisses him off. He collars me around the neck, and I'm ready to toss my head back into his nose and likely change all that "won't hurt me" smoke into "ass kicking" smoke, but Kai cups me under the chin and stops me cold.

"It's the only way forward for our people," she says.

The fight goes right out of me. I was ready to spirit her away. I had no contingency plan for if she wasn't in the mood to be spirited. Hos pulls me back, and I let him, too stunned. Kai follows a pace behind, her arms crossed over her chest, looking for all the world like a woman restraining herself. Chaco caws loudly from the black sky above, and the sound brings me to my senses so that I can hear what he has to say.

"I may have to leave you for a little while."

"What?" I say out loud, forgetting mind to mind entirely.

Hos looks strangely at me then up at the sky.

"You have to let him take the bell," Chaco says, as though that explains everything.

I jerk my arm out of Hos's grip and settle my hat, damp around the rim. I'm not looking to rile Hos up, but the way Chaco's talking scares me, and when I get scared, I get angry—mostly at myself. I'm the one that got everyone into this.

"This isn't your fault," Chaco says, from high above.

"I ain't a hundred percent sure what *this* is," I say out loud.

"It's a sacred ceremony—"

"Shut up, Hos. I ain't talking to you."

He blinks the sneer right off his face and looks up at the sky again. "You're talking to that thing, aren't you? I always knew you were a witch."

"If you're looking for witches, you probably oughta start with the man behind the fire."

"Dark Sky'll fix you right up," Hos says, smiling wickedly. "Then you'll see. Just like I did. Just like Kai did."

"Yeah, well, I got a few questions of my own for Dark Sky. Maybe we can all enlighten each other."

The heat in the summer hogan is intense. The fire is roaring like the wind is whipping it into a frenzy, but I can't feel a breeze. The smell of hot pine and baking piñon mixes with great gusts of sage smoke. The smell is overpowering, ultra pure, like someone spilled Pine-Sol.

Jacob Dark Sky is still shirtless, sitting against the thatched wall in the back of the hogan, slowly ladling water over himself from a wooden bucket between his crossed legs. His sightless eyes are open, staring out beyond the crowd, maybe even beyond the desert itself.

"Ya'at'eeh, Keeper. Welcome."

The desert floor shifts under me a bit. "How do you—"

"You were expected. You are not of the people, but you have a part to play in what will come. Remove your shirt."

It's all I can do to not clutch at the bell. Somehow, Dark Sky senses my hesitation.

"All who enter into the hogan must be purified, Keeper or not. I can sense your family near, in the in-between. They may come as well if they purify."

Chaco lands on the hogan and watches me carefully. He bobs his head up and down, tense and alert, like he's waiting for the right moment to cross a busy street.

I set my hat aside and pull my T-shirt over my head. The bell, as always, stays right where it wants to be, right over my sternum. When I was eight and my chest was as flat as paper, it stuck out a bit. Now, it rests in the dip.

Hos watches me warily and hands a mortar of pollen to Dark Sky, guiding his hands to grip it. Kai looks at the bell like never before. She's seen it many times, felt it with her hands, pressed it between our bodies. The way she touched it before was always with a sort of reverence.

Now, she just looks hungry.

Dark Sky takes a pinch of pollen and turns to the four corners of the hogan, dusting toward each. He sprinkles me with what is left, wiping a swath down the center of my forehead before clapping his hands free of the rest in the fire—literally in the fire, without flinching. When he turns around again, his milky eyes are on some horizon line above my head, but his hands are sure as he traces the leather down my neck.

"There it is," he says. "Such power for a thing so small."

Chaco watches Dark Sky's hands with careful tics of his head. When he gets to the bell, my bird is tensed like a runner before the gun.

"The bell is my charge," I say, but my voice doesn't come out as strong as I want it to. "I am its Keeper. Nobody else."

I'm ready for him to take it, but Dark Sky's hand falls slowly away. "The bell belongs to nobody. It is a tool, a key. One I will use, in time. But not yet. Our people have not yet gathered. There are four more nights in the Windway, after all. Much work to do."

I grip the bell. I can't imagine how I would feel with it gone. It's been with me for over a decade. The bell and my bird have taken up residence in the hole my parents left, the hole that Pap left. When everything was a blur of pain and fear, they've always been there.

Another thought from Chaco: *The power is in the giving of the bell, not the taking.*

I know what he's saying. I feel it too. But my brain just

can't make that jump. I don't know who I am without it. I can't just hand it over.

"Don't touch it!" I blurt suddenly.

Dark Sky pulls his hand back. He knows the same deep magic Chaco knows. And he smiles. "Fear not, Keeper. I won't take the bell. In time, you'll give it to me."

He tosses another sage bundle on the fire. "Now, we sweat. You along with us. Until the time is right."

"What is that thing, anyway?" Hos says, stepping closer, eyes narrowed.

Dark Sky turns to him and starts to speak, but I see my opening. Maybe if I can get him to take the bell, it'll turn the tables. It won't work right for them. It might protest, might send out some sort of distress signal. It's done stuff like that before.

You never know who's listening out there. Could be something gets through to Ben, even. It's worth a shot.

"It ain't for Indians," I say even though the word sounds ugly in my mouth.

"What did you say?" Hos asks, stepping closer.

Dark Sky clears his throat. "Sit, Hosteen. He's riling you—"

But I press on, interrupting him. "The last Indian that tried to touch this thing died in a tornado of crows. It ain't..." I struggle to continue, to sound like I mean it. "It ain't for your kind."

That hooks him. I can see it in the way his face changes. Wary no more, he settles into that old, familiar hatred, the kind he first found in high school and that likely got beaten deeper into him in jail. He's most comfortable mad, I can tell.

"You think you know us because you creep around the

Rez? Because you picked up a few Diné words? Do you know what *Diné* means?" he asks, his voice dripping.

"Navajo," I lie. "Or Indian or whatever."

Kai narrows her eyes. She sees through me. I just hope she can't see all the way.

"Hosteen—" Dark Sky says, more forceful this time. He tosses the ladle back into the bucket.

"Wrong, bilagaana. It means 'only human beings in the world.' We were, once. We will be again."

In one motion, he grabs the bell and yanks down hard, snapping the leather thong. I can feel it uproot, hear it, even. It's the sound of grass ripped from the soil by the handful.

I don't feel pain, not at first. But I know it's coming in that terrifying way a deep cut or a bad burn doesn't hurt when it first happens. The bell knows it was stolen, knows it's not where it's supposed to be. It vibrates with the force of the stealing—nothing big or loud, not like I saw when it formed at Pap's death. It's just a soft shudder that stretches out through this world and, I hope, even farther.

Mom and Dad snap into place next to me, Joey by Hos a second later. They look surprised, as though they didn't mean to step back.

"Not yet, Hosteen," Dark Sky growls. "Give it back. Quickly!"

Hos looks at the bell wide-eyed. He feels it, too, the shudder. He doesn't know what it is, but he feels it. He punches the bell back into to my gut, and I grab it on instinct. The second he lets go and the bell is in my grasp, the shudder stops.

Hos flicks his hand like he's been stung. Dark Sky holds out his arms as if to still the night. Everyone is quiet, expecting something but not quite sure what.

The silence extends. In the distance, the wind screams.

When still nothing happens, Dark Sky lowers his hands. "Fortunate," he says. "Very fortunate. Now sit next to me, Hosteen, and do not move. Our people are not fully gathered yet."

The sound seeps back into the night. Insects chirp and buzz and flutter. Hos moves over to Dark Sky in a daze, massaging his hand. He sits heavily, grabs the ladle, and pours water over himself before dragging the smoke to his face by the fistful.

Mom and Dad and Joey look back and forth among each other in shock. Mom holds her hand up, and there, in her open palm, sits her crow totem, skin to stone. Yet here she stands.

"What in the—" In a snap, she disappears again.

Whatever force called her and the rest back here, to me, against the force of the totem, is gone.

Dark Sky settles again, breathing out fully. "Just sweat," he says.

Whatever was supposed to happen, whatever we were expecting, I feel like I failed.

I look toward the sky for Chaco, a question forming in my head. "What did I miss?"

But Chaco is gone.

9

THE WALKER

I'm showing a very bitter old lady from Wales the way through the veil. I'm not totally sure what each newly departed soul sees in me when I show up, but I've been at this long enough to give it a pretty good guess. I think she's got me pegged for *yr Angau*, which is sort of like an unfriendly tax collector but for souls. In the legends out this way, each parish has one.

In reality—or what passes for reality in my day-to-day —it's just me. For everyone. So I'm in backcountry Wales right now. And also in high-country Wales right now. And urban Wales. And all over Britain. And in a big mess on a cruise ship halfway across the Atlantic that's best not to get into. I'm all over the eastern seaboard of the US as well. In the thick of it in Mexico. Don't even get me started about Chicago. You get the idea.

"Aye, aye," she says, scowling and tying a plastic grocery bag over her blue-tinged perm, "I know what they say: when *yr Angau* comes, he will no' go away empty-handed." She looks fondly out of the old, warped window of her living room, where she died in her chair, and for a second, she appears ready to impart some final rural-farmer wisdom. Instead, she says, "Still can't believe you didn't take that witch Doreen from down the block first. But here we are."

"I go where the soul map tells me," I say, waiting for her to settle her purse over her forearm before ushering her to where the veil waits just back of her puzzle table, rippling slightly in an unfelt breeze. She's within an arm's length when I hear a weird buzz. I can tell by the way she pauses that she hears it too. She even looks at me, questioning, but the veil rolls over her like a wave over a sand-castle, and she's gone before a word can leave her.

The veil stills, but that weird buzz doesn't stop. Now that I focus on it, it's more of a vibration, like a pulse. Sort of like feeling the whine of an old engine through the steering wheel.

"What the hell is that?" I ask the veil. Our conversations are very one-sided, but I still ask. I talk to the veil a lot. Because I guide more than a hundred people through the veil every minute, we spend a lot of time together. It beats talking to the wall, but not by much.

I wriggle a pinkie in my ear to try to clear the buzz, but it stays. I take a look around the room for the first time. The other hundred places I am fade to the background for a second, and I sense my body forming up around me for real. The sensation of being fully "here," even for a span of seconds, is so strange that I just thread my fingers for a bit.

I glance into a standing mirror next to the closet. My face is so chalky that it looks painted, and not your kiddo-birthday kind of face paint either but the real-deal ceremonial stuff, all thick from animal fat. My eyes are black pits. Their shadows stretch to the veins at my temples.

Before, in my time of living, I was dark, darker than most Navajo, I think. I'm having a hard time remembering exactly what I looked like then. I know I was a tribal cop, but I don't really remember my day-to-day. I've been so many things to so many people by now that it's hard to pick out the *what*s and *when*s of anything specific.

I think I might need to take some PTO.

The thought makes me laugh, standing in the sunken den of the dearly departed, shag carpet between my toes. This job doesn't come with PTO. Already, the soul map calls me. Another fraying thread on the great cosmic rope tugs at the back of my eyes. The tug will get worse, the longer I ignore it.

I dig in my ear again and swallow a few times to try to pop the sound. On the third swallow, I sense a type of pop, but the buzz remains. I recognize that pop. Something has come through to the soul map.

Chaco. His name has an odd, rusty creak in my brain.

I swirl a black hole in the room with my open palm, blurring the fabric of time and space in a living room that looks to have been frozen in time for decades. The soul map shimmers on the other side. I never flew in an airplane when I was alive, but every time I open the soul map, I imagine it's a bit like I'm high in the sky, looking down on an endless city—one of the big ones, Los Angeles, maybe, or Tokyo. But instead of streetlights and little moving cars and blinking bulbs on the rooftops, each light is a person's soul. Some of them pulse, some blaze, and some are guttering. All of them are connected, tied to one another as threads in a great rope without end.

Quite a few are nearly out. I'll be seeing them soon. But first, Chaco. And this damn buzzing.

I see him soaring toward my spot on the map, a dart of

black on black that's easy to miss, like a passing bat might blink out the stars.

"Well, well, it's my bird friend," I say as he flares his wings and settles on my outstretched arm. The pressure of his talons feels good—substantial, real, and strangely unfamiliar. "I thought you'd forgotten about me."

Chaco looks at me cockeyed, unblinking. "Are you serious? I was here three moons ago."

I try to think back. *Was he really just here? Did we talk?* I've been feeling a little out of it lately.

I try to laugh it off. "What's a moon, anyway? I swipe right, it rises. I swipe left, it dips back."

Chaco's not having it. "We talked about the Rez, remember? About a bunch of weird shit happening there."

"You sure it was me?" I ask, mustering a weak chuckle.

"No, it was the other embodiment of death that walks the soul map, snipping the last threads of the living," Chaco says flatly. "Walker, I know the job pulls you to a lot of places at once, man, but you gotta get it together. You're getting worse every day."

"I'm fine," I say, but I was always a bad liar, and I know it comes across like I'm talking out of the side of my face. I work my jaw around. That vibration is itching my ear something terrible. "What's this about the Rez?" I ask in a lame attempt to change the subject. "I was just there. Seems alright to me."

Chaco fluffs out in a big bird sigh. "No. You weren't. You haven't been back on the Rez in too many moons to count."

"That's not true. We just kicked Coyote's ass out there—"

Chaco puffs up and gets right in my face, and I'm

expecting to get a big, bad dose of bird snark, but then he just deflates, which is somehow way worse. "That was way back, buddy. Way back."

I try to remember. I have a lot of memories from the Rez, enough for a few lifetimes, even though mine was cut short there. A lot of them are rusty. And some—like this one of Caroline playing cards with me while I got chemo —I feel like I've gone over so many times in my head that I'm not sure what's real and what's not.

Caroline.

She's real. And she's a real reason I told myself I would stay away for a while. We let each other go. She had a life to build. I had a job to do. It was a good parting. Sure, I still feel a bit of a hole, but I only meant to stay away for a little bit, to help us move on.

I guess time just sort of slipped.

Caroline. And Owen. And Grant. And Joey.

I try to force myself to remember everything I can about all of them, and all at once, my brain spreads out in a nauseating double vision. Chaco is right. They aren't on the forefront anymore. I'm shocked by how dusty they feel in my mind. When I need longer than five heartbeats to come up with Owen's last name, I start to panic.

"Bennet," I say finally, huffing a breath. "It's Bennet." *But where does he work, again?*

And Grant, the Keeper, got the bell somewhere in Texas. I was there for it. But in my mind, that's like a set piece, a dark night on the desert. It could've been anywhere. I've been called to hundreds of thousands of similar nights in similar deserts.

"He's from Texas," I say.

Chaco looks at me warily.

"Midland. It was Midland. See? I remember." I scratch at my ear again.

Chaco shakes his head in a series of little tics. "Yeah, well, Grant *Romer* from Midland, Texas, needs you. The Keeper needs you, Walker."

"Well then, I'm going," I say. "Just tell me where."

"How about I take you there?" he says.

"I think I know my way to the Rez, Chaco."

He holds out his wings wide. "I'm sure you do. It's just that last time you said that exact same thing, then I lost you to the job for a whole lot of moons."

"No shit?" I ask. "Are you serious? I think I'd remember that."

Chaco perches on my shoulder, and I know by how good it feels that he's right. I haven't seen him in a long time. My mind is betraying me, but my body doesn't lie.

"That's the thing about forgetting," he says, pointing the way with his beak. "It sort of creeps up on you."

We walk the rope together, Chaco standing tall on my shoulder, but the space between is filled with questions I'm too afraid to ask. And answers I probably don't want to hear.

I CAN'T BELIEVE I forgot how good the Rez can smell in summer.

At night, everything smells like wet dirt for just a little bit, even if it doesn't rain. It's a sharp, clean scent that gets baked away in the high sun, come morning, but for a little bit at night, the rock and the creosote and the fine silt sand seem to breathe all at once. That's the first breath I take when I hit the desert floor, and I cough like a kid with his first cigarette, which is not a good sign. That means I really have been away for too long.

Also, I have no bearings. I feel like I once knew the whole eastern pan of the reservation like the back of my hand, from Gallup up through the Rez proper, all the way to where it pinches near Utah. Now, I try to trace all those old Indian roads in my mind, but everything looks like the soul map. IRR9 looks like the rope I walk. The washout roads around the canyons look too much like the smaller threads I trace out, each with a sputtering soul at the end.

We've arrived at a great gathering. We used to have these at the visitors' center, big exhibitions for the fire dance and the hoop dance. But this feels different. This is no tourist show. And this valley isn't somewhere tourists would park a rental. Pit fires light the far darkness at intervals, and I sense a hundred souls, maybe more, scattered between them. Other living things are near too—snakes, mostly.

I turn around and take in the main attraction, a very nicely woven summer hogan, the kind Gam and the elder twins used to sit under in the high heat of summer, back when Joey and I ran wild around the Arroyo, refusing to act anywhere near our age.

See? It's already coming back. Not sure what Chaco is so worried about.

Maybe it's the guy behind the hogan fire, the guy with the old-man face and the young-man body, looking right at me with searing blind eyes.

As if in answer, Chaco lands on my shoulder. He hasn't left my plane, which makes him as perpetually invisible to everyone in this valley as I am.

"What is this?" I ask, waving at the strange man. He

doesn't wave back, of course, but his white eyes shift in a way that makes my stomach drop.

"A Windway, supposedly," Chaco says.

I've never seen a Windway this big before, or this public. But maybe things changed since I died.

"He's a Singer, then. And that man there with him, he must be sick."

"Look closer, Walker."

Something about the sick man strikes me as familiar. He's built like a guy that works with his hands. His face has a shade of scruff on it, but I can see a little bit of a lost boy in it, too, around the eyes—one particular lost boy.

"Grant?" I ask, as though he can hear me.

He pays me no attention, of course. He's got one hand on his chest like he's been split open there, the other reaching out toward another Navajo, some prison-yard reject built like a fire hydrant. But that boy, that man, is Grant, alright. Grant in fast-forward mode. And he's lost the bell.

"Oh no," I say. I know I'm not exactly up to the moment, but I don't know what else to say. This is my home, but I also feel like a stranger, which is playing tricks on my mind.

"Closer, Walker."

The desert I'm supposed to know like the back of my hand suddenly seems like it's closing in on me. This is a thin place. The walls between worlds have been carved away here. Whoever this Singer is, he's a surgeon and not entirely at home in the land of the living.

I sweep the darkness, and I see my friends.

All eyes are on Grant. Owen kneels by him in an uncanny reversal of the boy holding the man on that godforsaken street off Menlo Park where the Coyote shot Owen three times.

Joey is there, too, warring with himself. I can see in his eyes that he wants nothing more than to beat his way through this mess, to leave a trail of broken bodies if he has to. Whatever it takes to get the bell back to the Circle, to the Keeper.

But he's holding back. He was always more level-headed than me.

And there, standing between the Singer and her son, the last line of defense, is Caroline Adams. She's older. I know that in an instant, and she's never been more beautiful.

She can't see me. I know that. Nobody can. But she's always been the closest to the other planes and to me. When she turns her head my way, her eyes drop a cold bucket of water over my head. She can't quite see me, but she knows I've come.

"Where were you?" she whispers, sadly scolding, like I missed the whole game while out back, wandering the stars.

"What is all this?" I ask in words she can't hear. The sounds fall flat on the dead side of the world, my side of the world.

"Help us," she says.

"I don't know how! I don't know what this is!"

The Singer stands. He's sweating like a horse, pollen running down his chest in rivulets. For a moment, I think he might see me. For a moment, I hope he does.

But no, he passes over me like everyone else.

Still, he senses something. My arrival always kicks the natural order off-kilter a bit. The snakes writhe in the shadows. The chant falters a bit. Talk drops off.

He breaks the silence with a powerful keening battle cry, raising his hands toward the night sky. "The Windway calls the old ones! And the old ones appear! All have a part to play in the ceremony…" He looks around, passing over me and back. "But not yet. Everything in its own time, Walker. You've been called too soon. In time, we will lead our people to their new home, together."

I lean toward Chaco. "What the hell is he talking about?"

"That is Jacob Dark Sky," Chaco says. "He has come to lead his people to their new home."

"Yeah I heard him. What the hell does it mean?"

"It means he's gonna save the Navajo to death. Unless you can do something about it." Chaco nods at a girl that looks torn between standing watch at the fire and going to Grant. "What do you see when you look at her?"

I assume he's asking what I see aside from a very pretty Navajo woman. So I look deeper until I find her on the soul map. Her thread is there, but the color is all wrong. A strange, hollow white creeps along it, slowly, like it's been dipped in a bucket of bleach. The threads of the others gathered here are much the same.

"It's like… like her thread is being rewritten," I say.

"And Dark Sky?" Chaco asks. "What do you see in him?"

For one thing, white smoke pours from his eyes in the thin place. Where it touches, it lingers. The smoke could very well be the bleach. His thread is tied up in the map same as all the others, but it's scaly and black. The way it's woven makes me think he's trying to hide how long it's been here, like a snake tucked in its den.

"I see a lot of shit I don't get," I say. That's all I *can* say.

"But you're right—he's doing something to these people here, changing them slowly."

"He claims to be a Singer from the Colorado Creek clans, doing a big heal. That's all," Chaco says, flatly.

I've heard of the Colorado Creek Navajo. They're an interesting group. On the one hand, a lot of people say all Navajo are of the Dinétah, the people, no matter where they live. That's my mom's way of thinking. On the other, the hardliners say only those who live in the Dinétah are Navajo. It's a tricky thing.

But I think I would've known if our Colorado Creek cousins had blazing white eyes that could pierce the thin place and a Singer with this kind of pull. Gam would've said something about that, for sure.

"I guess they don't make 'em like they used to over at Colorado Creek," I mutter.

"Maybe, maybe not. Or maybe something got through and is hitching a ride on Jacob Dark Sky," Chaco says.

"Got through? From beyond the veil? But that's not possible. I man the veil."

Chaco clears his throat and side-eyes me good.

"Oh," I say, taking his meaning. "Shit. I let this guy through?"

"I'm not saying that," Chaco says. "But you didn't *not* let him through. Or it. Whatever it is."

What Chaco doesn't say is that I'm all over the place and spread way too thin and dropping the ball, that I'm losing a step.

"Chaco, I had no idea—"

"Don't worry about what happened, Walker. Only about what's happening right now. And right now, Dark Sky is changing these people, severing their ties to this place. Now, why might he be doing that?"

"Because he's going to take them away," I say softly.

The Rez plays a key part in the balance between the lands of the living and the dead. This place, the Dinétah, is a place of power, sort of like a massive thinning. All things are linked here.

To explain how important this place is to us Diné would be hard. Imagine your favorite chair, the one you always sit in, the only place you really feel comfortable. But instead of finding this chair at a chair store after sitting in a lot of chairs—you were actually put in this chair by the gods because this chair is the origin of your existence.

It's sort of like that.

Anything that would try to sever this tie is bad stuff on a lot of levels. Also, the Dinétah without the Diné is just land. If this place became nothing but desert, the loss that would inflict on all the worlds is hard to comprehend. It would set off a terrible unraveling.

And it's not something I'm gonna let happen on my watch.

"Alright then, so it's bad. We can deal with bad. How do we kick his ass out?"

"No idea," says Chaco.

I look at him sidelong.

"I got no idea, man," he says again.

"Alright. Forget this," I say, rolling up my sleeves. "Okay, Mr. Dark Sky, time to head on back to whatever unholy plane you walked out of."

I focus on his thread. A black thread is a dead thread, as far as I'm concerned. And a dead thread can be snipped.

Chaco flares out his wings as if to drag me to a stop. "Walker, wait—"

"See ya never, Dark Sky." I form up the ol' snippers with my right hand and reach for his thread with my left.

I get about one foot from the serpentine strand connecting this thing with the great beyond before a hellish wind kicks up out of nowhere. A gust like I've never felt in this plane or on any other rises in a blink at slaps me right off my feet with the speed of a snake strike.

I fly back twenty or thirty feet and land on my ass. I'm not hurt, of course. My hurting days are long behind me, except in the pride department. Chaco is battered back like a plastic sack. He picks himself up awkwardly.

"We tried as much," Chaco says, preening himself straight again. "Joey came at him head-on as soon as he set up this chant. Similar results."

I stand up and set my shirt straight, pulling out the collar again. "Well, that's just great. So, what, we just let him do whatever he wants?"

"No, we do not," Chaco says emphatically. "You gotta figure out how he got in, and you gotta figure out how to get him out before he brain-drains this whole place. These people are Arroyo—Heartsblood of the Rez, in case you forgot."

That stings. "And how am I supposed to do that? Ask him out for coffee? I can't touch him, bird."

Chaco shakes himself like a wet dog and settles back on my shoulder. "I think I have an idea." He shivers again. "But I don't think you're gonna like it."

As if I needed any more reasons for the dropping sensation in my gut, when I turn to him again, he won't meet my eye, not even one of his patented Chaco side-eyes.

"That bad, huh?"

"Things have a way of coming around again," he says

like he's talking to himself. "She knew it better than anyone. The land. The seasons. The wind. Even the people. I think I've felt this dark wind before."

Whenever Chaco starts muttering to himself, that's a surefire sign he's about to drop some uncomfortable knowledge. Either that, or he's having a low-level panic attack.

"Slow down. When?"

"Naba's time," he says, "when I went by the name of Blackfeather. Naba managed to get rid of this wind."

Talk about dust on a name. I don't think I've ever heard Chaco speak it before. The sound is so strange coming from him that I need a minute to realize he's talking about my grandmother. My family all called her Gam, but she was known outside our circle by her clan-given first name, Manaba. The old-timers at the Arroyo called her Naba for short.

With time blurring around the edges like it is for me these days, I sometimes forget that before Chaco rolled with Grant, he rolled with Gam, Keeper and crow, for decades. Of course they saw some crazy shit, maybe even something as crazy as this.

"That's great! We'll just do what she did!"

"I don't know if we *can* do it again," Chaco says softly. "I'm not even totally sure what it was she did."

In front of me, in the living world, Caroline does her best to calm Grant. Her touch, her words, they seem to be working. Gam had that power too. She might not have been able to smooth smoke like Caroline can, but she had other balms—food, among them. A long time has passed since I thought of my grandmother. Finding her face in my memories is hard.

"So we're screwed," I say.

"Not necessarily. If this is a Windway, even a modified one, it'll take a while."

From what I remember, that checks out. "Could be three days. Or five. Maybe even nine. All depends. But yeah, at least a few days."

Chaco bobs his head, and I can't help feeling he's also trying to psych himself up for what he's about to say. "Okay. Okay. So that leaves a little bit of time for us to figure this out."

I try to spin the wheels in my brain. I've got to be able to do something. I'm the literal manifestation of death. I can walk back time. I can—

Wait a second. I can walk back time. *I can walk back time!*

"Chaco, I'll just walk her thread back. I mean, she lived for a long time, so I'll need some pointers from you on where to start. Give me at least a decade to work with here—"

"It was when Ana died," Chaco says, which shuts me right up real fast. My heart hasn't beaten for years, but every time I think of my sister, my ribs feel like they're squeezing it anyway. That's probably why I try not to think of her all that often.

Then again, if I couldn't feel that squeeze, the space between Ana and me—me and everyone else—would only grow. The veil is such a thin thing, but at the same time, the two sides couldn't be farther apart, as opposite as day and night or noise and silence.

I've avoided the threads of that time for all my dead life. Living through it once was painful enough. Plus, it hurts to look back on a time when I could hold people and feel like it meant something. Everything I touch on this side feels like a shadow of itself.

Chaco shakes his head. "You can walk back the thread, but it'll only show you what happened. You gotta know what Naba was *thinking*."

"You know as well as I do that ain't part of the job description."

"Not yours," Chaco says.

This time, I'm the one looking at him sideways, stretching the silence in that way Gam perfected, until he goes on.

"For me, knowing what the Keeper is thinking is part of the territory. My kind, the thin things, it's sort of what we do, especially when we've been paired."

In the living plane, the big ex-con-looking fella and two of his thickest associates are herding Grant, Caroline, and Owen to a spot on the canyon floor just outside the hogan. The big fella is stripping a pine bow and gathering up a shallow bowl of pollen. They steer clear of Joey, for now. But all my friends are essentially trapped here. If they run, they've essentially handed over the entire crowd to whatever twisted plan Dark Sky has.

Plus, Grant doesn't look like he's going anywhere without that girl—Kai is her name, I remember now—and nobody is about to leave Grant.

Sorry, folks. Looks like it's up to me.

"Let's put an end to this," I say.

"Open up, then."

I'm all squared up to swirl open the map and go hunting for answers, so Chaco's words literally trip me up. I stutter step a bit and look his way. "Say what?"

Chaco's streak of red feathers flashes as he stretches tall on my shoulder, and out of the blue, I'm hit with a memory of myself looking down from the lip of the far side of the Arroyo after one of those big snows where the drifts might build up to ten feet. Joey's already jumped, of course, and he's egging me on with every sort of insult designed to make a thirteen-year-old boy do something stupid.

I can almost hear myself muttering, "Don't think—just jump. Don't think—just jump."

Chaco shivers. "Time to see eye to eye, Walker. I said open up. Quick, before I lose my nerve."

I'm not putting two and two together, and I guess when that happens, I sometimes get a slack-jawed look. Chaco comes right at me. Before I know what's happening, he's stuffed his head into my mouth. I can feel his arrowhead shard of a beak, hard and sharp, on the back of my throat. His feathered crown slides along the roof of my mouth. I reach up to grab him on instinct, but he's already down to the wings. I stagger backward, feathers slipping through my fingers. He uses the top of my hand as a springboard, his talons clawing forward until somehow that enormous bird is *inside of me* and I'm on my back, heaving for air on reflex even though I haven't taken a real breath for years.

The feeling is how I imagine drowning to be: an enormous rushing in the lungs, a strange settling sensation, a weight where no weight should be. My sight wavers then fails, and now I'm blind, screaming voicelessly as I fall.

When I hit the snow, something clicks in my brain, and I'm thrown outside myself.

I watch myself sit still for a moment, taking stock. I landed hard on my arm after that jump. I remember that now. I can see myself testing it out then giving Joey a tentative wave. I can see Joey too. He's about four feet from where I landed, stuck in snow up to his ass and laughing like a maniac. *How could I have forgotten this memory?* It's so clear. Like... like I'm living it again.

I'd say he's more of a Morning Rock than a Dejooli. But it is what it is.

The thought comes unbidden to my brain in one-hundred-percent fluent old-world Navajo. That's strange because my Navajo sucked back then. I was always searching for words, cobbling together sentences when I had to, but this thought comes naturally. It's an old family joke. *Dejooli* means "up in the air" in Navajo. And I just very clearly fell on my ass in the snow.

Morning Rock was Gam's clan, passed down from her mother's side to Oren, my dad, but that's where it stayed. I got Dejooli from my mom, and Gam often poked a bit of fun about how I may be Dejooli in name, but Morning Rock never really fades.

In fact, the voice, the tone, the thought itself, all of it is exactly the kind of bone-dry, desert-flat humor Gam used to have.

The realization dawns upon me slowly, like sand sliding down a mountain. My eyes and ears and even my thoughts are not my own. I've been blown to the past and set in the passenger's seat of someone else's memory.

Gam is the one driving now.

10

MANABA MORNING ROCK

Some days, I don't know if I should slap that boy or tie him to my waist with an old horse rope. *Jumping off a ledge like that...* It doesn't matter how much snow came last night. Even twenty hands of snow won't save you if you jump on the old car Bly Bodrey's worthless son pitched over. Or any other piece of trash still down in that canyon, disguised under the whiteness.

But the old Arroyo magic holds, and my grandson lands in a puff of snow, as does his friend, Joseph Flatwood. Both of them are laughing like it's the deep of summer and not the days of ice. And of course I knew this. No grandson of mine will come to harm within the four mountains of the Dinétah, not while I live.

"Nice jump, Bennyboy!" Flatwood says. His voice is strong and full even when made smaller by the canyon and the packed snow.

I grumble. *A bad influence, that one.*

My grandson, who they call Ben—a white man's name I had no say in—is a little red dot in a big white world. I knitted that red hat, knitted it to fit his wild head of hair, to keep him warm in the days of ice. I sang when I knitted so that he'd have strength when he wore it.

My grandson looks around, proud as a rooster that he threw himself off a rock like an idiot, then he sees me standing at the lip.

"Oh shit," he says.

Sometimes, people think that just because I won't speak the white man's tongue, I don't understand the white man's words. They think wrong. I know, and I understand, and *oh shit* is a good white-man phrase for this.

"Grandson," I say in Diné.

He's a willfully ignorant child when it comes to our speech. He could learn and speak better than anyone, but he won't. I blame his mother's influence. Sitsi told him to focus on speaking English, said that was the future for him. But she has never understood that without our past, there is no future for the Diné. In that way, the past and the future are the same.

I also blame his father—my son—who can't stay sober for one night to care one way or another.

Even from up here, I can see Joseph Flatwood swallow when he looks at me.

"You better go, man."

I know that phrase too. Joseph Flatwood is a petty criminal and an all-around troublemaker. When your parents die young and leave you, you become a trouble-maker. He'd likely be dead if he hadn't been brought back into balance by his grandfather, an Arroyo man himself, one of the old blood. Now, I think Joey understands the old ways even better than my grandson. But he's still a troublemaker.

Such is the balance of things.

My grandson climbs back up to me using a thin path cut through the snow. Then he stands there and looks everywhere else to avoid meeting my eyes.

"You're supposed to be helping your sister with her schoolwork. Instead, you're trying your best to break your neck."

I watch him as his mind works out the words, the patterns of speech, and pieces together the meaning. He's a bright boy. He understands enough.

"Ana's back from the hospital already?" he asks, eager now.

I see how much he loves his sister and try not to let my pain show on my face. I am very good at feeling the pain but not showing it. My son Oren was good at this composure as well, at first, but now the pain is often painted on his face. I fear it will be the same for my grandson soon enough.

It is good to feel the pain but also good to face it with composure. Otherwise, it threatens to overcome us.

"How...?" He struggles to form the question I already see on his face.

He wants to know what the doctors in Albuquerque said about Ana and if she is healing.

"Your father will tell you," I say.

And what he will say is not good. If one believes the white man's medicine is the only way to heal, that is.

My grandson's face falls. He knows. That's part of the reason he's here, throwing caution to the wind, along with himself. Like all people who leap off cliffs, some small part of him wishes for a bad landing, to be snuffed out in an instant. For my grandson, that means to be taken away from the realities of Ana's condition.

Our Arroyo has many cliff jumpers. Even if they don't

necessarily jump with their bodies, they do it daily in their minds. It wasn't always this way. Long ago, the Diné were masters of the land, from the tops of the mountains to the bottoms of the valleys. Then we treated with the white man. *Now look.*

My grandson starts toward where Oren waits in a truck the same dirty-snow color as the Arroyo roads, engine rattling, tailpipe puffing into the sky.

Joseph Flatwood knows better than to get his rear end within striking distance of my boot, but the way he stands at the lip of the drop and watches his best friend go, wringing his cold hands in his pockets, takes away the rest of my anger. With the anger gone, the fear steps forward again. That's all anger is—a mask for fear to wear. It has its purpose, but wearing it is tiring, and I am an old woman.

At the truck, Ben turns back. "Aren't you coming?" he asks.

I shake my head. "I have business here. I will be home to cook dinner."

Ben's face falls further. He knows what I think of what the Arroyo is slowly becoming: a den of snakes when it was once a circle of stones. That I have business here bodes ill. He catches Flatwood's eye, and his friend nods in encouragement. Flatwood loves my grandson like a brother and Ana like a sister. When someone loves your family that way, it is hard not to love them in return.

So yes, I love Joseph Flatwood like a grandson.

But he's still a troublemaker.

As Oren's truck rolls away, Joseph comes up to me. "Let me walk you to them, Grandmother," he says, using the honorifics. Unlike my grandson, his spoken Diné rolls like water.

I nod, allowing it. Joseph leads the way, trekking carefully down a well-worn path back to the Arroyo proper. I notice he kicks the trail free of snow in places and stamps it down in others so that I may walk more easily.

"So how is she?" he asks, still facing forward.

"Their medicine did not help her. Whatever the Albuquerque doctors were hoping for, it did not come to pass."

Joseph sags. But to his credit, he keeps moving. I remember him as a newborn, a child I helped to deliver in the quiet of the high summer moon. His mother screamed in labor but still constantly asked if he was healthy and would be strong. She was a woman worried for her child before he took ten full breaths. She was right to worry. Both she and Joseph's father left the Diné way, and when they did, the protection of this place failed them. But Joseph remains. His grandfather is a true Diné, old and stubborn, but even the oldest among us eventually fall back into the earth. Then hard choices are coming for Joseph.

I place a hand on the center of his back, and he flinches. Then he straightens, never stopping.

"There are other ways," I say.

His nod is reluctant, the nod of a young man obliging the old. After all, I am not much younger than his grandfather. Joseph and Ben and all in this coming-of-age generation have the least faith in the old ways of any I've seen.

My crow wheels above like a drifting break in the sky. Joseph sees him too. It is hard to miss a bird as big as he is. He has gone by many names and will go by many more, but I call him Blackfeather.

"You were right," says Blackfeather to my mind.

"Another body, in a washout at the Blackwater basin. An Arroyo woman."

His voice is how I remember my own grandfather's, one long, soft stream of sounds in my mind. I do not answer. When I was a young Keeper, I talked all the time. Mostly, I listen to Blackfeather these days.

"She was shoeless, wearing nothing but a shift. She froze to death. The Walker still has not found her."

The Arroyo is losing people. The exodus started as a trickle but is getting worse. Each is the same, like they're possessed by a desperate need to leave this place behind. What they do not realize is that when they do, they make all of us weaker. Each loss chips away at the whole.

"Struck by the same madness, then," I say.

Blackfeather is silent this time. He is not Diné, not in the sense that he was born of the people of the plains. When the bell first came to me, he had a strange foreign accent, but now he understands the power of silence as well as any in the Dinétah.

Blackfeather wheels overhead, and I walk in silence for a time, watching each white puff of breath from Joseph as he leads a way I know by heart.

Eventually, Blackfeather puts words to my thoughts. "The wind is gaining strength, chipping away at all four peaks, but it is the worst at the Turquoise Mountain."

The four sacred mountains form a hedge of protection around our land. They provide us with strength, hope, a sense of place. If that protection fails, the people will lose their way. If the wind breaks the Turquoise Mountain down, the Walker will find more than a handful of desperate Diné who have given up hope and fled.

If the Walker finds them at all, that is.

I know better than to ask about the Walker. Even

though Blackfeather can cross the realms and land on the shoulder of death itself if he so wishes, years have passed since he has seen the one who walks the soul map.

And that is the real problem, to my mind.

"And my granddaughter?" I ask.

Blackfeather often checks in on her for me, and I want to make sure she is settled back home.

"Ana is sleeping," says Blackfeather, "but her sleep is closer and closer to death."

My bird does not mince words. I know in my heart this is true, but hearing it is still hard. I have tried to speak with Ana about the Walker in a way she can understand. We call him Black Bear in our stories. He sleeps and sleeps until his time comes.

I can almost hear the air split around Blackfeather's beak as he wheels high then cuts low. I remember when the bell first came to me and I was a young-blooded woman, Blackfeather dove like one of the gods had taken a knife to the sky and let loose a sharp shard of darkness. Only later did I notice a hint of dark red beneath, as if a streak of war paint is hidden behind the feathers. He has only grown more beautiful. Or maybe I've just grown old enough to see it.

Joseph pulls aside near the hogan line.

"Good luck, Grandmother," he says, looking up at Blackfeather, who flares his wings like a living shadow and settles on the simple trailer of the elder twins.

He walks away, buffeted here and there by the wind, but he keeps his feet. Life has thrown much at Joseph Flatwood, and he has stayed standing. I fear life will throw a good deal more before his time here is done. Certain forces here hate that kind of strength and are drawn to it with the goal of tearing it down. The prize for standing tall is more fighting.

Tsosi and Tsasa have lived together in this trailer at the far edge of the Arroyo ever since I can remember, and I can remember well. They haven't always been old, but to my mind, they were never young. My earliest memory of them is attending a Blessingway chant at their hogan— last in the long line out on the flat beyond the Arroyo. They were taught by the same Singer as me, long gone now, who apprenticed to Standing Pine himself. I sing well, but the elder twins have twice the voice, and the gods tend to listen carefully when they call.

The cinder block stairs leading to their front door are well swept and washed clean of the winter dirt. Same with the fake daisies that line the flower boxes to either side, their yellow bright against the gray midday.

The door is always open. The inside is as small as expected and as cozy. An electric space heater at the end of the narrow passage to their bedrooms ticks softly. The elder twins get cold easily, yet they insist on sitting by the firepit out back for hours a day in every season. Part of me thinks the reason is to show solidarity in these times. The Arroyo has lost many since the wind started to break through.

Both men greet me when I step out back. "Ya'at'eeh," they say, their voices deep and strong even though they take some time to push themselves up from those ratty camper chairs they sit upon. Both walk around the fire to embrace me as we were taught by Standing Pine, pressing forehead to forehead. They offer me a seat and wait while I settle my coat around myself.

Blackfeather lands with an elegant hop and steps to my side, where he puffs himself into a black ball and roosts. The fire seems to take notice of the bird and gives him its warmth in greeting. The elder twins nod welcome. He sighs a bird sigh.

For a moment, we four are silent. The fire laps at the dry pine. More dry pine sits under a tarp between the twins. I have no idea where they get it in the dead of winter with snow on the ground, but the elder twins take care of the Arroyo on the spirit plane, so the Arroyo takes care of the elder twins on the living plane.

Usually, I never break the silence first, not even with Ana, who is very good at what she calls staring contests. But this place is different.

"Blackfeather found a second body, the woman from the Arroyo Mud Clan," I say, careful to avoid her name out loud lest the Chindi hear. I grab a pinch of pine ash from the edge of the fire and toss it into the air, just in case. I gently wipe my fingers clean and resettle them on my knitting bag. "The same sickness took her. Her spirit still walks the foothills."

The twins nod as one.

"Old Black Bear breathes heavy tonight," Tsasa says.

I believe the elder twins knew about her death even before Blackfeather knew. They were the ones who suggested he sweep the western edge of the Dinétah, at the foothills where the shadows begin.

My part said, I settle into the chair and bring out my knitting. The sky is heavy above, but the clicking of the needles calms me. I'm making Ana a sweater and placing as much of my song within it as I can, but the going is slow. I have learned that when the balance of the land of our people is at stake, I tend to skip a stitch now and again.

Tsosi clears his throat, a slow rumble like a lazy engine turning over. "May I ask Blackfeather a question?"

My needles pause. The elder twins passed the bell to me. They know much about the thin world and the world beyond, but they usually talk around Blackfeather, acknowledging what he is—the power he has as a thinning—without actually addressing it. Talking around things is a time-honored tradition of the Diné.

Blackfeather looks up at me and I down at him. He sighs another bird sigh.

"Of course. He is always listening."

Tsosi turns to the bird directly. Blackfeather cocks his head to eye him straight on. "Ya' at' eeh, thinning called Blackfeather."

Blackfeather nods.

"When was the last time you spoke with the Walker?" he asks.

Blackfeather ponders, the firelight reflecting in his obsidian eyes. "I do not know."

"The bird does not know," I say, in turn. "Blackfeather may sometimes have dealings with the Walker, but he is not tied to him as he is tied to me."

The twins settle back as one. They look at each other for a moment before Tsasa grabs another pine log and tosses it square upon the fire with an expert touch, kicking a vortex of sparks that swirl in the dead light of the afternoon before vanishing. The gray of the day is battered back a small amount by their passing.

"Has Blackfeather ever told you about where this Walker came from?" Tsasa asks, brushing his hands gently down the grain of the buckskin throw that covers his legs.

Blackfeather says, "He is simply one more human in a long line, eternal until the ringing of the bell replaces him. I do not care who he was before, only that he does his job. Shepherd souls to the veil and keep the balance."

I look up at the elder twins and clear my throat. "No. He has not. Do you know?"

The twins glance at each other.

Tsasa pulls his throw higher over his legs. "In the passing of the bell, a story was told that he is one of the Athabascans," he says.

I furrow my brow and take up my knitting again. The repetition settles my mind when I am forced to think outside of time. The Athabascans were the people from which the Diné of today came, ancient stewards of the land who lived hundreds and hundreds of years ago.

Blackfeather clears his throat also, a croaking sound that fits the gloom well. "That strikes me as true. When I saw him last, he was receiving a death in a pasture of the western Great Plains. He said it was his home. He pointed out a great valley where he said his family had learned a technique to farm corn for maize in six of the eight seasons."

I know much about our people. No Diné has called a great valley in the western Great Plains home in recent memory. The white man has boxed us in for generations.

I turn to the elder twins. "Blackfeather hasn't spoken with the Walker since our ancestors walked the Great Plains freely and called it home."

Blackfeather tics his head to the sky and blinks rapidly. "Can that be?" he asks me.

The bilagaana think of time as a series of doors to open and close behind them, moving in a straight line from here to there. For the Diné, time is a great circle. Everything has a season. Life, death, rain, snow, planting, harvesting—all things come again. The balance offers peace, but one can easily get lost within the circle as well, until one day, they wake up blinking like Blackfeather, looking around at a land completely changed, wondering what has been lost and what has been forgotten.

In the distance, the wind cries as it is split in two by the Turquoise Mountain. When I was young, after I was chosen to apprentice as a Singer, I went on horseback to the Turquoise Mountain with my mother. The mountain is called Tsoodził, which means "strong tongue." We sat at the foot of the sacred mountain and prayed that I would be given the strength I needed to sing for my people. I remember the way the top still glinted with snow, and from a great distance, the whole mountain glimmered true to its nickname: Blue Bead.

That was long ago, and I remember the wind singing with joy then. The sound is different now, more a ripping sound than a true song.

The sacred mountains are strong, but this new wind is relentless. I picture bits of Tsoodził chipped away every day, its power scattered to the sky one bead at a time until the cornerstone that anchors the south of our land is reduced to a lump of rock and our people are unprotected from whatever the wind blows in.

The elder twins look to the south, as if they've read my thoughts.

Tsasa stirs the fire with a pine bow so lacquered with resin that it shines near black. "The wind batters the sacred mountains. The Walker forgets this land. These things are connected."

Blackfeather stirs at my side, and I translate. "He does not mean to forget," I say.

Tsasa stops stirring and looks my way. "No one *means* to forget."

The warmth grows, and I blink away a sudden weariness, putting more force into the knitting to stay awake.

Tsasa settles his stirring stick back at his side. "Two nights ago, when the wind blew in the great snow, my brother and I had a shared dream."

Blackfeather stands and looks at me. I reassure him with a soft brush of his crown.

"A dark sky to the west. A man riding the wind with white eyes that burn," I say.

The elder twins quiet as one. Tsasa resettles his hands, one over the other, but the trembling is unmistakable.

"I had it too," I say.

Tsosi shakes his head sadly, sucking at his teeth as if the fire between us had misbehaved. The elder twins know as well as I do how powerful shared dreams are.

"So it is true, then. Something approaches from the west, something that the sacred mountains would normally keep out, something that draws the most desperate of our people even to their deaths."

The wind screams, the sound distant but penetrating. I fight the urge to plug my ears, as if that would give whoever, or whatever, is causing this assault some sort of victory. I pick up my knitting instead.

"Blackfeather and I will go to the mesa at Knifepoint and see what there is to see," I say, not looking up.

Those that hold to the old ways believe that First Man pinned Tsoodził to the earth with a knife. Few know of the very spot, but my mother was one of them. She showed me, about halfway up the mountain on the side facing the Dinétah. If something is trying to unravel the sacred mountain, that is where it will do its work.

The elder twins nod as one. Perhaps this was their plan all along. They are strong Singers, but their hiking skills are not so strong these days. They never were. Tsosi and Tsasa prefer their firepit. They travel by telling the stories and legends of our people.

Tsasa pushes himself standing. He walks wordlessly to the back stairs and slowly climbs inside. Steps seem to be taking the elder twins a bit more time these days, and they aren't alone. When he isn't busy throwing himself off cliffs into the snow, my grandson has been building a ramp with a banister up the simple stairway to our home. He is doing this without asking, perhaps knowing that if he did, I would swat away the thought that in time, I may be having trouble getting in and out of my own home.

But there is enough strength in me yet.

When Tsasa reappears at the back door, he carries a crow feather tied to a lump of turquoise the size of my thumb. I've only ever seen the piece during the unraveling when the twins sing. It is powerful protection, given to them by Blackfeather.

He brings the feather to me and sets it gently upon my knitting.

"Keep Blackfeather's protection here, cousin. I have the bird himself."

Tsasa sucks at his teeth as Blackfeather stirs softly at my side, turning an eye toward the ground. "This wind has an evil sound. It will focus on the thinning. It may be hard for Blackfeather," Tsasa says.

My hand moves to rest against his broad outer wing, to reassure myself he is still there. After a moment, I loop the fetish over my head. The crow feather settles over the bell like a cupping hand.

Tsosi tosses a fistful of dried sage onto the fire, and the burst of smoke seems to mute the keen of the wind for a time—but only a short time.

"Look to the Story of the People," says Tsosi, watching the sage smoke billow away. "The answer is there, even if we cannot see it yet."

Tsasa smiles fondly at my knitting. I've had to patch the sweater I made for him countless times.

"Look within as well," he says. "You always hum the same song when you're knitting yarn together. Perhaps it will work to knit together the mountain as well."

So many places to look. Look outside. Look inside. To the Diné Bahane', the story of our creation, and to the Turquoise Mountain of today, which the white man calls Mount Taylor. "Is there anywhere I shouldn't look, cousins?" I ask, unable to keep a wry smile from thinning my lips.

Both men laugh. It's a good sound, defiant, but it soon fades. Our gazes return to the fire. Nothing more needs to be said, least of all what I know passes unspoken between all four of us.

Time is short. And we may already be too late.

11

THE WALKER

Riding along inside the mind of my dead grandmother has me feeling very queasy. Or maybe that's just Chaco mucking around in my ghost guts, making all this possible.

I hear him chime in from nowhere and everywhere. "You still with me, Walker?"

"I don't know who I'm with," I say, "or where or when." I take a few deep breaths to try to fight down the sudden sense of vertigo hitting me as I see Gam's life unfolding as it did twenty years ago out of my left eye and this Windway from hell out of my right.

"You gotta stop thinking about time as a line, man," Chaco says—or Blackfeather or whoever he is right now. "You are here and there and everywhere, but you're still you. Remember that."

Grant is still here, too, surrounded by family but trapped. And not by Dark Sky or Hosteen Bodrey. He's trapped by Kai. None of them are restrained in any way I can see—but her very presence is a type of handcuff all the same, one Grant clicked on himself. He's determined to bring her home.

I see the hogan fire for what it is now. In the living plane, it is a ceremonial firepit, cut pine resting on a bed of simmering coals that smokes high into the night sky. But in the space between, it is a roaring bonfire of white wind that bakes the desert ground to cracking. These cracks run underneath all the Dinétah. And if you followed them, I bet you'd end up at Knifepoint on the Turquoise Mountain, the anchor my grandmother fought to save.

"Are we too late?" I ask. "Is the anchor already broken?"

Dark Sky is threading his white smoke around everyone like puppet strings. He's staying clear of Grant, Joey, and Owen for now but only because Caroline seems to give the white smoke pause.

The bottom line is that I failed. I'm not Gam. I'm a bad Navajo. I let my own backyard go to shit, and now it's come back to haunt me, and I'm gonna get the entire Rez wiped out.

Chaco chimes in from behind my eyes. "Your grandmother thought she'd failed too."

"But she did it. She sang it back. I can't do that. For one, it can't hear me. Nothing in the living world can."

I feel Chaco holding something back.

"What aren't you telling me?"

I feel him guarding his thoughts even as he says, "She did whatever it took, Walker. That's all you need to know right now. But she didn't do it alone. She had help from the feather and from her friends."

"The Walker doesn't have friends. This is a solo gig."

Chaco scoffs. "Get over yourself. You don't really believe that."

I look at Caroline and Owen, together with Grant, each drawing strength from the others. I look at Joey, who seems half an inch away from throwing what little caution he still possesses straight into that hogan fire and going after Dark Sky himself on whatever plane he can for as long as he can hold up before the wind or the desperate crowd takes him down.

"Look closer," Chaco says. "Around his neck."

The feather. Joey wears the crow feather around his neck. The hot wind flutters it lightly against his chest.

"She gave it to Joey," I say. "But when? I think I would have noticed if—"

"We're wasting time, man. Every second Dark Sky sings, his power over this place—over these people—grows stronger."

"Okay, fine," I snap back. "Joey's got the feather. So what? We don't even know which mountain is failing. It could be all of them."

"You know which one."

And I do, of course. Turquoise Mountain. All things come again. And I also know I'm only pissed at Chaco because the time has come to make a decision that will force the people I love to act, and they only have to do it because I screwed up at my job and let this thing in where he shouldn't be.

The only thing that stings worse than screwing something up badly is having to watch other people clean up my mess, people I love.

"It'll take all of them," I say. "Joey for sure. But Grant, too, with the bell. Caroline and Owen as well. They'd

never let him go without them. All right. Let's do it. Whatever needs to be done. You and me."

"About that... I can't go," Chaco says. "I couldn't then,
and I can't now. The wind breaks me down, blows me off
course." His voice gets smaller for a second. "Believe me,
I've tried."

I wait for more, but Chaco doesn't give it.

"Well, that's just great," I say.

"It is what it is. I wish it was different."

I look around myself, helpless. My hands ball into
fists. I try to focus on the problem at hand just like I used
to when I got thrown curveball after curveball as a cop
with the NNPD, but I can't keep a single line of thought.
I'm here at the Rez, but I'm a hundred other places every
second, too, and I used to be able to do this—do everything at once—but now, my brain feels like a well running
dry.

Panic blows across my body, hot then cold like the
desert wind, and I'm reminded of a snapshot of my living
life when I felt this way before. I was at my desk in the
station, giving a written statement about that terrible
night when Ana disappeared and Joey ran. I was doing my
best to piece together the timeframe when an awful pressure built up in my brain. I remember trying to focus on
the task at hand, but the focus just wouldn't come to me,
and the same thought occurred to me then that occurs to
me now.

"Chaco, I don't think I'm doing so great... in my brain."

I really want to hear Chaco reply with some wry
comment that I'm imagining things, maybe to feel the soft
weight of him bop against me in that way he sometimes
does that says, *Chill out—you're fine.*

Instead, he says, "We can deal with that later."

And his voice isn't quiet, exactly, or sad, really. But it's careful. It's very careful. And in that second, I know I'm right.

I'm losing my mind. Slowly, yeah. But it's happening.

The moment has a clarifying effect, as though by admitting it, I push a little bit of the panic away. I've had my problems, both alive and dead, but I've always owned up to them.

Chaco steps carefully to the front of my mind, like he's walking down a cracked and pitted sidewalk. "Right now, we need to get all four of them to Knifepoint on the Turquoise Mountain."

Focusing is hard. I have to pull a lot of myself back from all points of the globe, which is a bit like getting dressed with my eyes closed when I'm pissed off, which I am. My job did this to me. My sneaky shit job has been taking bits of me away from myself all this time, boiling my brain by degrees.

I take several deep breaths, calculating distances. *Think of the logistics.* Caroline, Owen, and Joey could phase there in an instant, but not Grant, and they won't leave Grant. Mount Taylor is at least an hour and a half away.

"How are we gonna get Grant there?" I ask.

Chaco stops at the pit of my chest. His weight shifts me forward a bit like a runner at the starting gate. "He can handle that truck of his pretty well," Chaco says. "He'll get there fast enough. If he can outrun Dark Sky and this mob."

One look at Grant says as much. He has a look about him even now that reminds me a lot of Joey. Both of them want to turn the tables here, and they want to do it now. They just don't know how.

"That kid would've had a great time counting coup

with Joey and me back in the day," I say. Of course, he isn't a kid anymore and hasn't been for some time. I wonder if this is what parents feel like when, suddenly, they snap back to reality and find themselves clapping at their son's graduation or crying at his wedding or packing up the car to send him off into the world.

"We need a distraction," Chaco says, and I feel him climbing up inside me.

"Wait!" I gag, scratching at my chest. Choking aside, having him in there wasn't so bad. The company was kinda nice.

"I can't go to the Turquoise Mountain, Walker," he says, at my throat now. "But I can make a distraction."

I dry heave as his feathers slide against the back of my tongue.

"Help them if you can," he says. "It will help with..."

With my fractured head. My lost time.

I try to ask how I'm supposed to do that, being dead and all, but all that comes out is a rattly gasp.

Chaco perches for flight, his claws braced against my lower teeth. "Good luck, Walker."

Then he launches from my mouth.

12

GRANT ROMER

The bell knows it was almost snatched away. It feels heavier now, like it wants to sink into me. Warmer too. It gets like this when things are happening just outside of our sight.

Dark Sky's words still ring in my ears. *"When the time comes, you'll give it to me."*

Hos is staring bullets at the bell and at me. He's still holding his fingers like it stung him where he grabbed it, but he looks like he wants to try again anyway. Only Dark Sky's orders keep him seated.

Dark Sky knows what Hos doesn't. The bell only works right when it's given freely. Anyone who takes it messes up the balance. Shit breaks.

When Chaco vanished, Dark Sky smiled. He moved back to his sandpainting like that was all the evidence he needed that he had everything figured out. He's carefully sifting black sand into the jagged outline of a snake, singing to himself in a low rumble while sweat drips from his brow onto the painting.

He sure as hell looks pleased with himself. Confident that whatever signal the bell sent out fell on deaf ears. He thinks the danger has passed. But he ain't lived with the bell, not like me.

If he did, he'd know the danger never really passes.

Dark Sky said the bell is nothing but a tool. That I may be the Keeper, but it isn't mine, and maybe he's right. But that's only part of the story. I may not own the bell, but it sure as shit owns me. That's what people don't realize about this whole arrangement.

Once the secret of what this thing can do gets out, the Keeper is never safe. Nobody I love is safe either. All we can do is run when we have to. Lay low when we don't. It happened with the agents, and it happened with Coyote, and every time we get out of trouble, I think maybe we're home free.

We ain't.

I look carefully into the faces of the people I love, boxed right in here next to me, and I can't help wondering if each time the bell brings trouble down, they think of me a little bit less as Grant and a little bit more as the Keeper.

Or in Kai's case, maybe she's not seeing me at all anymore. I try to tell myself that's because she's not right. Dark Sky has her under some sort of spell, something cutting her ties to me. But fire can't exist without smoke, and the bell hanging around my neck simmers day after day. One day, that look Kai is giving me now is how Mom and Dad and Joey and everyone will look at me.

I won't be Grant anymore. I'll be the Keeper. And that's it. The world needs a Keeper more than it needs a Grant. And the world gets what it wants.

I know I'm spiraling. Usually, my bird talks me back up, but even my bird up and left me, and this bell is getting so damn heavy. That witch fire in the middle of the hogan pulls at it. The black bear totem sitting in the coals grows brighter and brighter, and all around us, the night gets heavier. Only Dark Sky seems immune. He nods to himself as he finishes the snake piece of the sandpainting and moves back to the bowls that make up his colors.

Joey sags and shifts to his other knee. Mom and Dad lean against one another. Hell, we don't even need Hos and his squad to keep us here. Pretty soon, whatever magic Dark Sky is weaving will trap us here just like we were chained to the desert floor.

"Fine time for Chaco to go on a joyride," Owen mutters, wiping his brow and unbuttoning his collar.

"He was here," Mom whispers. "Ben. I felt him."

"Maybe," Joey says. "But if he was, he's gone now."

"So we're status quo, then," Owen says. "Wonderful. Nice of him to drop by. The problem is we're still trapped inside a crowd that some cult leader has induced to mass psychogenic illness."

"These people aren't crazy," Mom says. "They're... detached. The color of their smoke is bleeding out, turning white."

"Windway or not, Dark Sky calls upon the gods," says Joey. "I think the gods are coming."

Dad rubs at his temples. "This is textbook mass hysteria. Just like the Dancing Plague of 1815. That's all."

"Can't it be a bit of both?" Mom asks, placing a hand on his.

Dad looks at it and her and at this whole place like he's totally lost, like the desert he's crisscrossed in the Old Boat for over a decade just shifted under him and he ended up somewhere he has no business being.

"No," he says. "Not for me. It can't be stress-induced

hysteria brought on by ungodly living conditions *and also* a magical group abduction. It's the former." When Mom presses down gently on his hand, he pulls it away. "And I'll tell you why. Because what I see in all those people, I've been seeing here in some form or another for ten years."

"Soothe the symptom," Mom says, seeking Dad's eyes again, trying to pull him back in. She waits for him to finish the routine I've heard them toss back and forth countless times, but he won't.

So I do. "But treat the cause."

I know what Dad's thinking. He gets like this when he feels he can't help. When he reaches into his doctor's bag of tricks and comes up emptyhanded, he doesn't know what to do with himself. We all spiral in our own ways. I want to tell him that he doesn't have to be a doctor to make a difference here. He makes a difference every day just by being Owen, by being Dad.

But when I try to speak, the bell gets really heavy, and I grab it reflexively. It's hot in the way that tells me to keep my eyes open.

"Somethin's comin'," I whisper.

At first, the hogan gets really quiet. Dark Sky stops singing. Even the fire seems to pull down on itself. My eyes water. I work my jaw and swallow hard, and when my ears pop, I can hear something, the distant sound of beating wings, coming from everywhere and nowhere. It gets louder and louder until the line of firelight just beyond the hogan bends, like two giant fingers pinched the black horizon together just for a second.

A thin, black line rips the air then twists in on itself until it becomes Chaco, fully extended, wings as wide as a desert vulture's, comin' at us like he had a football field worth of running room. The size of him, the sheer force of him hitting the air, bowls back damn near everybody.

Only Dark Sky seems unfazed.

He rises from sitting cross-legged in a single, fluid motion and opens his arms, smiling like a lunatic. "You can try me, Thinning, but you know you will break against me. I am almost as old as you."

I reach out desperately to Chaco with my mind, aiming to tell him not to do it, to say there's gotta be another way. He needs to know that I'm sorry I thought he left me, that I know he's always there when I need him most.

I aim to tell him that I love him.

But in the moment, no words come out, only a choppy yell that's all of it and none of it at once.

Chaco's voice overpowers me anyway, and I only hear one thing, bouncin' like an echo down the canyon.

"Get everyone to the Turquoise Mountain."

I flinch at the strength of the words in a voice I've never heard him use before, like one of his old voices from another time. It's a command.

He's careening toward Dark Sky, and the crazy Singer seems to grow broader before my eyes. The wind kicks up around him, and I know he's right when he says Chaco is gonna end up on the bad end of this fight. I scream out warning in both thought and word and reach for him like I might be able to catch him before he breaks against Dark Sky, but before he hits, Chaco dives.

He dives straight into the fire. His talons rip through the sparks and hot white coals and rake angry red lines in the baked sand that glow like fired steel. He grabs something, the black bear totem. In the explosion of fire and smoke, it seems to roar in his grasp, but his talons are sharp and cinched like knots as he leaps high, wings beating a downdraft that scatters the sparks as he passes right over Dark Sky.

"Run!" he shouts in that same ancient voice, then he bursts into flames.

I don't know how long I stare at him flaming in the sky. I know that the one thing I don't do is exactly what he said I should—not, at least, until Joey grabs me under the arms and pulls me away from the hogan like some sort of frozen doll, heels draggin' in the dirt. And still, I watch. I can't do nothin' else.

You think when get somethin' precious taken away from you, somethin' you really care about, that you'll scream when it happens. Fight for it. Rage against it. Maybe it's your mom or dad, maybe your wife or kids. In the dark nights, worst-case scenarios run through your head about how you might lose everything. That's your brain preparing best it can. Putting you in that headspace like a test run, but a test run is just that. Pretend.

When terrible things *actually* happen, like when Pap got knifed by those agents that awful day a lifetime ago and I saw the only blood family I had left die in front of me, my body took the loss, not my brain. And that isn't something you can prepare for. The brain practices no-contact, but the body is in the game. You learn that the first time you get hit.

The day the agents killed Pap, they also tried to kill Chaco. But Chaco is a hard thing to kill. He's a lot more than just a bird. So even though they broke his neck, he eventually twisted it right again, and since then, I thought he'd be with me forever. That nothing can kill him.

I was wrong. The only thing that can kill Chaco is Chaco. If that's what it takes to protect me, to protect the bell.

He's a beacon of fire in the sky, something out of another time, more dragon than crow. He drips burning feathers. Each wingbeat throws a gout of flame into the blackness. Blue fire races up his broad back as he soars higher and higher until he's lit up from beak to tail feather.

He gets smaller and smaller, falling into himself like a spent wildfire, and I know he's going away, leaving me for real. Any idiot watching sees that, and everyone is watching. Dark Sky, the Bodrey camp, hell, probably the whole Rez is watching. But that's not how I know he's dying.

It's his voice. His voice has always been there even when he wasn't talking to me, like a hand resting on my shoulder. I never said it out loud, but Chaco was the best part of the whole Keeper thing, by far. Chuck the bell, but let me keep the bird.

That voice is getting softer. That hand is getting lighter.

"Time is a circle," he says, his voice clogged with a strange tone that some way-back part of my brain recognizes as pain.

"Everything comes around again," he says.

I can't take my eyes away from this great flare out in the sky even as Mom keeps me from stumbling face-first into the dirt as we run down Crooked Snake.

"I love you," he says—this, faintest of all.

I have no words for him. I'm too afraid to speak. I owe it to my friend to watch, even to the end.

And when it comes, there's no bang, no explosion,

nothing like when Chaco broke into this world. He goes higher and higher, and I'm running down a dirt road lower and lower until what's left of him punches into the great black sky.

He joins the stars, and I lose him.

It's as awful and as simple as that.

13

CAROLINE ADAMS

I've got a love/hate relationship with crazy. When things go from zero to sixty in an instant—like, say, when one minute I'm trying to comfort my son and safeguard the bell, trapped front and center at a big Navajo sing, and the next, a giant bird blows into reality and turns itself into a flaming torpedo right in front of my eyes, and everything goes to hell in a handbasket—that's what I'd call crazy.

Half the crowd ducks and covers, half the crowd watches, stunned. Kai and Hosteen and his flunkies are all wide-eyed, frozen in place, trying to figure out what's real and what isn't. Even Dark Sky seems like he's on his heels. Most people are when things fall apart.

But most people didn't work as a floor nurse. We hate crazy, but we kind of love it too. It's when we really get to work.

When Grant screams for Chaco, it takes everything in me not to let my heart break right next to his. When he reaches out like he wants to grasp the flaming crow, maybe to pull him back and burn up right along with him, I almost do too.

Then Grant says, "Get everyone to the Turquoise Mountain." He mumbles it, really, through lips bent by sorrow. I don't even think he hears himself say it.

I don't know what the heck it means, but I don't have to. All I know is that it's from Chaco, and Chaco wouldn't do a thing like torch himself without a very good reason.

When I worked on the oncology floor at ABQ General, things would often go from asleep to five-alarm fire in an instant, sometimes two or three times a night. One minute, a patient is watching daytime soap operas on a tiny TV in the top corner of a room, and the next, they're coding. Machines start to beep, then alarms go off. Pager phones buzz. The whole floor jumps into motion. I've spent years running toward messes. This is no different.

I turn to Owen. "Now's our chance."

But of course, Owen is already on it. Back at ABQ General, he was usually the one calling the shots if he was on call when things hit the fan. He straightens now like he often did then. I recognize a bit of confidence returning to him, and I wonder when, exactly, he started losing it.

"Where did you park, Grant?" he asks, his voice sharp. The way he talks when he's trying to bring people around again.

But Grant is watching the black space of sky where Chaco went and doesn't seem to hear anything. Owen cups Grant's rough cheek and turns him face-to-face, and I'm struck by an outline of the two men in my life that, in the firelight, looks like something from a different time.

"Son," he says, kind but firm, "where is the truck?"

Grant blinks, comes back to himself a little bit, and

points somewhere up the valley. "It's at the turnoff. Bottom of Crooked Snake."

Owen holds out his hand. "Give me the keys."

Grant fishes his keys out of his pocket and hands them over, dazed. He keeps turning to the retina burn in the sky that was Chaco.

Owen turns to me. "I think he needs help only you can give. Can you and Joey get him to the truck? I'll meet you there."

I nod. He leans over and kisses me on the cheek, then he grabs his totem and blinks away. The feel of his lips lingers for half a second, and I get a teenybopper urge to reach up and hold the spot on my cheek, but we have no time for that now.

Joey looks like he wants to punch his way out of things, which is one way, but not one I think I'd be great at. I can't phase without Grant, and I can't give Grant my totem because Chaco warned us against bringing the bell into the thin place. He's big on rules.

Or he was.

I push that thought away too. Bottom line is we can't phase our way out of this, so we've gotta do it the old-fashioned way, hoofing it.

With the black bear totem gone, the weird wind that kept the fire at the center of the hogan in a controlled blaze breaks down with a low *whuff*, like a huge sheet of plywood thumping to the earth, and the blast of air nearly bowls the front row over, us included.

Joey helps us upright. Bowling Joey Flatwood over would take a lot. He shoves us toward the path back up to the trading post and says, "I'll buy you time."

Grant staggers forward and seems to find himself just a bit. "Chaco said everyone, Joey. That means you too."

"Trust me. I'll be there. Get to the truck." His face bends into a warrior's scowl, his braid gleaming in the firelight. The wind plasters the feather to his chest. Then he blinks away.

Somewhere behind us, Dark Sky bellows, "Keeper! You cannot stop what's coming! You've only made it harder on yourself!"

I think of those searching tentacles of white anchored behind his eyes. Chaco may have scattered them for a bit, but I bet Dark Sky gloms them back together again soon enough.

I brush a hand over Grant's head, the way I used to when he was a kid. His eyes are hollow. A great chunk of him is missing with Chaco gone. I can almost see the hole it's blown through him, which is why it kills me to have to say, "Mourn later, honey. Run now."

He nods and staggers forward into a trot that I soon have to work to keep up with. He looks back to check on me, and a memory hits me, of when he was just a little boy with a bird on his head and Owen and I were the ones looking back, checking to see if he was keeping up.

The wind gathers strength. The real wind. I can feel it streaming around me.

"You cannot run from what is coming!" Dark Sky screams.

I can't help but glance back. He's standing before the sandpainting, streaming black sand from his fist. The wind skips off the ground and kicks up the entire sandpainting as one, holding it in midair for a moment like a weaving suspended in the sky by a great invisible loom. Dark Sky thrusts out his hands, blind eyes open to the sky, and the sandpainting explodes in a tornado of color. "Our time in this world has come to an end, Keeper," he says. "These chosen Diné will pave the way to the next."

A ground swell spins me sideways, and I catch sight of Dark Sky in the center of a frenzy of color. Every last grain of sand has been sucked up and spun out from the jars and cups surrounding him.

"But don't be afraid," he says. "All will follow, soon enough."

He nods to Hosteen and Kai and says something that looks a lot like "Bring him to me."

Grant doesn't let me hang around long enough to figure it out. He pulls me back around by a shoulder. "Phase to the truck! I can climb out of the canyon faster than you!"

He's already bounding ahead, assuming I'll do exactly what he said. And he's right. I should totally be phasing right now. He's a strong young man, no stranger to manual labor, used to navigating the weird footing of these high-desert canyons. I'm more than a little out of shape and basically forty, no stranger to mac-n-cheese, used to navigating to and from patient rooms in a health clinic. But I have a crow totem, of course, so I can be anywhere.

But I'm afraid to.

Grant is about twenty feet up by the time he realizes I'm still climbing on my own two feet. He narrows his eyes in that way children do when they know something is off with their parents. He could never hide things from me for too long, and it makes sense that the street goes both ways.

"What's wrong?" he asks.

Nothing's *wrong*, really. But that's the whole problem. There *has* been a change inside me. Ever since I've been staring at those pregnancy tests then shoving them in the back of the cabinet very unpeed upon, something *has* been changing. I have a place inside me, deep inside, that wasn't there before. This place is tailor-made for someone special to grow, but that someone isn't there yet, so it's more like a hole. And what I'm realizing right now, with the worlds getting very thin and a terrible storm riding in on the wind, is that I've never wanted anything more than to turn that hole into a nest.

I feel fragile there, in the not-nest, desperately fragile and maybe already broken. I've triaged miscarriages before, in nursing school. The most heartbreaking part is that the life inside of those women was snuffed out weeks before they realized it. They've had celebrations and made plans and lived in the headspace of mothers, then they come in for a routine check. And I know that when I phase, I'm leaving the flesh-and-blood world, the warm world that a spark like that would need, and I'm walking closer to the dead world, where these beautiful sparks are ended before they can ignite.

I wonder how I'm supposed to tell all this to Grant, who's looking down at me with gathering concern.

"It's not good for me to phase right now," I say, huffing a little harder than I should as I catch up to him and push him forward again.

He goes reluctantly. "Why?"

"You're just gonna have to trust me. Your thing is the bell. My thing is the crow totem."

We're halfway up the ridge when the pressure drops. A vortex of desert sand and bleach-white smoke starts a slow spin on the flat below, gathering like a dust devil. Dark Sky is in the center.

A group emerges from the swirling, coming straight toward the path after us. The sand and smoke obscure them, but one of them looks tall and thin like Kai, and another has Hosteen's thick lumber. They carry big flashlights that pan up the path.

As if we needed any more encouragement to get moving, something rattles ominously from under the lower lip of the hacked-out steps at our feet. Only one thing on this planet rattles like that, and we both know exactly what it is.

I'm not a fan of snakes, but I feel like my dislike is of the pretty standard kind. If they didn't move so fast and lick at everything and have fangs, I might be on board. Grant, on the other hand, is terrified of them. His fear rolls off him in yellow waves like pollen squeezed from a pod.

"Get behind me," I say.

"Mom, that's a rattlesnake. Don't move. I can't see it."

But I can. All living things have a smoke, even snakes. Theirs is a sludgy purple. If you get bit by a rattlesnake, you have about half an hour to get help before your blood starts turning to sludge. That's the color of their smoke. Blood sludge. I don't tell Grant that, though, or that I can see maybe twenty of them within a stone's throw of the one actually rattling.

"Get behind me, Grant Romer."

He normally would have argued with me, playing his I'm-the-most-adult-of-us-all-now card. But the full name is high-caliber Mom ammo, and he does what I ask.

If a thing has smoke, I can calm that thing. It's what I do. Now, I've never done it on snakes, but I've done it on a lot of people that are a bit snake-ish, including the agents back in the day, so I go out on a limb and start walking, with my smoke sense out and ready to smooth.

Sure steps, I tell myself. *Confident steps.* That works for a bit. Then someone yells just below, and the flashlights snap to us.

Another dry rattle goes off within striking distance of my shin. I own cowboy boots, a cute pair Owen got me in Santa Fe way back when we had some money, but I am not wearing those boots, of course. I am wearing a pair of very not-snakebite-compatible Keds because, believe it or not, I did not expect to be doing a trust walk through a field of rattlesnakes today.

The snake rears back, the fangs dripping a putrid, oily smoke, but before I can gross myself out, I settle my own smoke upon it. I sort of envelop it, like dropping a double handful of flour on the countertop, and its tail stills. It's not suddenly my snake buddy or anything, but the revved-up animosity melts away quickly, which tells me it possibly shouldn't have been there to begin with. Maybe it has something to do with the ceremony below, the same way it seems to have cast a spell on everyone.

I pull Grant along quickly, catching each flicker of purple snake smoke the second it appears and smoothing it over with a drive-by rolling pin. Soon, we're really moving, taking the hacked-out stairway up two at a time. I can see the firepits that mark the top of the path and the trading post beyond. I think we've even lost the mob until I hear Hosteen Bodrey yell from below.

"There! At the top!"

The flashlights snap to us again just as we stumble over the top lip of the canyon. I shield my eyes and chance a look back. Hosteen and Kai are about halfway down, coming up quickly. She's climbing with a creepy, fearless speed at the crest of this dark white sandstorm that seems to have expanded out of the canyon, crawling up the sides, wreathing her and Hosteen and coming for us.

The canyon below is a disaster, flickering firelight crackles like an electrical storm underneath whirling clouds of sand. I can't see Dark Sky, but I know exactly where those tendrils of smoke are coming from. Turning away from that mess is easy. Ahead is the darkened trading post, lit in harsh relief by a fat white moon that seems to sit so low that I might bonk my head on it.

Grant stumbles ahead. "This way," he mumbles, threading a path between beat-up old cars and trucks, drunk with grief.

We squeeze between car doors and knock against side-view mirrors until we can take off down the slow curve of road that leads down to the turnoff. At the gate to the pass, I hear scrabbling from behind. The Bodrey group is up and out. Their flashlights gleam through darkened wind-shields and dance along the dirt road.

Hosteen's voice carries over the wind rising from below, harsh and guttural. "If I can't rip it from your neck, bilagaana, maybe I rip your neck from your body, huh?"

I guess jail didn't improve his manners much.

We make it through the gate, still chained wide open for the masses. We're home free until Kai's voice rings out, small but clear and more than a little witchy.

"You can't outrun the wind, Grant."

Grant looks back—I don't blame him. Heartbreak flushes his face. I know it because I've been there. All I can do is pull him into a hug.

Not long ago, Grant had a tentative foot in the Navajo world because of Kai. He knew he'd never be Diné—never be a true-blood Navajo like he wanted, from the day he met Joey—but with Kai by his side, he could at least come close, as close as anyone. Now, that same girl—who used to sit so easily next to my son, her long legs draped over his on that ratty couch of ours in the A-frame, the silence between them so simple and true—is chasing him away.

"That's not her talking, honey, not the real her. The wind changed her. Took her smoke away. And it'll take ours, too, if we let it. Then Dark Sky has you and the bell for good."

What he wants with the bell is still a mystery to me. But sometimes, when that code alarm rings, you gotta run on gut instinct. My gut says to do exactly what Chaco told us to do—get to this Turquoise Mountain before it's too late.

Doors slam. A truck just back of the trading post roars to life. I can't see it clearly, but I know from the sound and the way the lights blaze to life as bright as the sun that it's likely Hosteen's big custom thing. I remember passing it on the way in, the one with those obnoxious elephant-ear side view mirrors. The good news is that he's definitely parked in. *Small miracles.*

I urge Grant on, gently, and he joins me. We hit the curve and start gaining some downward momentum when I hear the first *crunch* from behind.

Grant and I look at each other, wide-eyed.

A loud snap echoes off the rocks then a squeal like nails raking down metal. A window pops, and something gets run over with the sound of a huge tin can getting crushed.

Hosteen is railroading his monster truck right through the crowded parking lot, paving his own way. But that's crazy because Hosteen loves that truck more than anything. Any time I have the misfortune of seeing him out in the Rez, he's usually holding court in the stupid thing. No way he'd wreck it of his own accord.

But that's not Hosteen, not really.

The engine behind us roars over a solid *thunk*, like a train car connecting. Another shattered-glass pop.

We pick up the pace, running way faster than is safe down a thin dirt road in nothing but the light of the moon. The engine roars again, and this time, the tires grab with an angry *whrrr* of thrown dirt. He's bullied his way through.

I really should have put "run down by an obnoxiously large pickup truck" a few notches higher on the list of ways I might kick the bucket as soon as I decided to make Chaco my primary residence.

But I hear something else, too, a horn honking rapid-fire from down the road. We're absolutely reckless in our downhill running now, and I feel like my legs are just barely keeping under my body, but even reckless running isn't going to save us from the truck that swerves around the bend behind us. That damn thing has enough lights to flag in an airplane, and all of them are pointed at our backs. Our shadows are thrown way out into the desert, stretching long and black, and that's when I see Grant's truck, just at the turnoff, and there in the driver's seat is Owen, inching it forward and honking like a maniac in a Fourth of July parade.

I start skidding to slow down as Owen reaches over with a long arm and pops open the passenger door, ready for us, and if we had maybe another ten seconds of head-way, I think we might have made it. But outrunning a truck is hard, even when I'm reckless in Keds. And by now, I can feel the heat of Hosteen's high beams, and all I can hear is the roar of whatever monster he has under that hood.

My panic brain has a strange conversation with itself. *He's not actually gonna kill us. He's not that far gone.*

And I tell myself again, *That's not Hosteen Bodrey. Not entirely.*

Grant splits away from me, hugging the inside of the road as a decoy, and I hear the tires shift, spattering dirt away, to follow him. *Brave and stupid.* I'm going to have to have a very stern talk with him once we cross the veil.

Hosteen is going way too fast to stop in time, at any rate. I doubt he even sees Grant's truck at the turnoff. I scream something unintelligible even to myself, as if I might explain over all the noise to Owen that he needs to gun it and to Grant that he needs to get to the far side, off the road entirely, but he doesn't have enough time. There's never enough time.

Grant trips on a section of washboard dirt and tumbles shoulder first, and I know that even if Hosteen *doesn't* mean to kill anyone, he just might do it anyway, and I utter an absurd screaming prayer that maybe that idiot boy lifted his truck so high that it might pass right over my son like I've done with a hundred little squirrels and bunnies in my time.

But Grant is no squirrel. Nothing is gonna save him except—

I hear a *whoosh pop*, and Joey is there, sitting right between Hosteen and Kai in the front bed of that monster truck, there in a blink.

And in that split second, when Hosteen registers that a stranger is between them, Joey whips the truck's steering wheel hard, right toward the mountain.

With another *whoosh pop*, Joey's gone, but the truck fishhooks like some big hand just slapped it across the hood. The grill bounces high off the inner gutter of the road and runs itself a good ten feet up the hill until it's almost vertical, and there it stops, shining in the moonlight as if it was just dropped there. I fully expect that thing to flip, but instead, it slides backward and settles awkwardly on tires that are apparently too big to fail.

Whoosh pop. Joey is beside Grant, picking him up, throwing him into the rear seats.

Whoosh pop. Joey is beside me. "Quickly," he says, pulling me by the crook of an elbow toward the truck, way more calm than he has any right to be, especially since he literally phased into the center of a speeding truck, which is pretty much the equivalent of jumping out of an airplane and parachuting into a teacup.

I'm still slack-jawed as he buckles me in and closes the door before jumping into the back cab next to Grant.

He slaps the back of Owen's seat. "Gun it!"

Owen doesn't need to be asked twice, especially because Hosteen's truck is somehow spinning its wheels again, trying to claw itself back to the road.

Owen punches the gas and manages to wrestle a gut-dropping skid under control until we settle on the packed dirt of the reservation road. Soon, we're on a straightaway, shooting south under that same fat moon.

14

OWEN BENNET

I'm sitting at the base of Crooked Snake, tapping my thumb on the steering wheel of Grant's truck a mile a minute and trying to physically manifest Caroline and him so that we can get the hell out of this place.

I know this might sound strange, considering I'm pretty much the only person I know who has crossed the veil and come back to the side of the living to tell about it, but I'm not exactly a spiritual man. My life revolves around patching up the flesh-and-blood side of humanity. Do that long enough, and at some point, you start seeing everyone as walking assemblages of vital organs in slow decay, nothing spiritual about them. On my worst days wearing the white coat, I would come home convinced humanity is nothing but a game of attrition.

Feeling helpless comes with the territory these days. I felt helpless when my family was stuck in that hogan before Chaco did whatever he did to shake some sense into everyone on his way out. And I'm getting that feeling now, waiting, eyes on the rearview mirror, fingers thrumming on the outer door like I've got the booze shakes.

They should be here by now. Grant being a bit farther back, maybe I can understand. He's got the burden of the bell and no totem, no Chaco now. Just his own two feet. But still, he's in better shape than I've ever been, and Chaco gave him a big head start. I saw that sandstorm kicking up when I phased out, and they were ahead of it.

But where is Caroline? I took precisely one quarter of one step to get to this truck. She should be right behind. *Unless...*

Unless she can't phase for some reason.

Maybe I should phase back and check on things. But knowing my luck, they would arrive the moment I blinked out and would be waiting for me while I'm looking for them, and we would be jumping back and forth, missing each other in some ridiculous Laurel-and-Hardy routine.

I lean out of the driver's side window and listen for any sound of them. I think maybe I hear a car start way back up the pass. Or maybe that's just an echo from somewhere else. This country is strange like that. I check my watch out of habit, as if we'd done some sort of synchronizing beforehand like we're robbing a bank. *Okay, listen, when the flaming crow bursts on the scene, we've got five, maybe ten minutes to exit the premises...*

But of course, no planning could've prepared us for this sort of thing. We have no playbook whatsoever.

Helpless.

I unbutton the second button down on my shirt, which I almost never do, and turn the air vent toward myself. Something is wrong. I'm not a praying guy, but if there was ever a time, this is it. Even if praying does nothing but give the illusion of helping when a person is really just thinking, at least it's doing *something*.

God, if you're here and you're available, maybe you could help my family get off this damn road...

Any god worth his salt would see right through me, I know. That's foxhole faith, phony as heck. I'm the guy that walked through the veil and fought with Coyote then came back and spent the next ten years trying to convince myself that a thing like the veil is really nothing more than a force of nature, more akin to a moth passing through a chrysalis than a spiritual experience. *Nothing to see here.* Never mind the fact that I was shot three times and the bullets came back out. I've had them in a little jar on my desk for so many years that I stopped seeing them.

Days like this make me wish life was more like a lipid panel. Either you're in range, you're out of range, or you get a warning. Backed by science. Clear action items to follow.

I slam my hand on the horn, not caring how it shatters the night. I do it again and again and again, and when it stops ringing in my ears, I hear a sound like a rockslide coming down the mountain. And behind that rockslide, perhaps even chasing that rockslide, is something that sounds like a freight train—a freight train with high beams rounding the bend.

I stick my head out the driver's side window again and see Grant and Caroline running down either side of the road as fast as I've ever seen either of them run, but I know in an instant they're not going to be fast enough. Hosteen Bodrey's truck is going to eat my family, and I can't do anything about it because at the speed he's going, I won't even be able to get Grant's truck out of the way, and it'll eat me next.

I kick the truck into reverse. Maybe somehow, some-way, I can get between them. I stomp the gas. The truck spits dirt in a cloud of red that billows up around me, and I know I'm not going anywhere fast enough, but I'd rather die trying.

Whoosh pop.

I hear it over the mayhem. I would recognize that sound even if I had a chainsaw blaring next to my ear. It's like Caroline's laugh or Grant's *Hey, Dad*, which I could pick out from a million other *Hey, Dad*s.

The high beams whip to my right, and I hear a big *whump* followed by a bunch of smaller *whump*s, and when the retina burn clears, I see Hosteen's truck hanging onto the side of the mountain and Joey Flatwood standing in the middle of the turnoff, helping my family to their next seconds of life.

I laugh, unable to help myself. Unable to do much else in the face of such things, I just laugh and open the passenger's side door. Caroline almost overshoots the truck then pulls herself back. The heat of her is wonderful. She radiates as she wipes her dripping forehead, smearing fine desert dust from temple to temple as Joey buckles her in. She's breathing deeply, but she's breathing. That's what matters.

Joey opens the rear cab and helps Grant in and through before slapping the truck and yelling, "Gun it!"

I whip onto the main road and drive like my life depends on it, which is a very real possibility, given what I've just seen.

Caroline is pressing her face to the vents. They're cranking out more cold air than any twenty-year-old pickup truck has a right to, but the temperature is still hot —hot inside, hot outside, and dusty. A red-sand miasma floats in the cab.

"Are you okay?" I ask. "What happened?"

She rests her forehead on the dash and sucks in the cold. When she turns to me, exhaustion is in her eyes, red dirt dusted across the freckles bridging her nose, the freckles I love the most.

"I had to help Grant," she says, still panting, "get through the snakes."

I check Grant in the rearview. He's guzzling from a big jug of water he keeps in the back. Always prepared, my son is. I'd like to think he gets that from me, but I feel ass-up these days.

"There were snakes? Plural?"

He nods and wordlessly passes the jug up to Caroline. Grant is very good at knowing when not to talk. I know enough to know when not to press. My family is in the car with me, and I've got Joey here as well, and none of them appear to be bleeding on anything, so that's good enough for now.

When we hit our first straightaway, I see high beams way back in the distance.

Joey turns his head, following my eyes. "It's them," he says.

"Could be anyone. There were a lot of cars," I say, trying to keep a little optimism up. If I can't offer anything else, maybe I can offer some dysfunctional optimism.

"It's them," Joey says again then straightens his back and closes his eyes. He starts to breathe deeply.

"Not a great time for a nap, Joey," I say. "That thing has a lot of horses, and this one is…"

"Watch it," Grant says wearily. "This is my baby."

"And it's a good baby, but it took its first baby steps off the Ford assembly line when you were negative one years old."

Grant rubs the roof. "Don't listen to him, baby. Just get us to the Turquoise Mountain."

I press on the gas and say a small prayer for whatever poor armadillo might be trundling across the road up ahead. *Two prayers in one day—look at me, a regular man of faith. Or maybe* heretic *would be a better word.* Pagan? *What do you call someone who's following a crow's orders to get to a Turquoise Mountain?*

"Is that the plan?" I ask. "Just hoof it to... Where the hell is this Turquoise Mountain, anyway?"

"White people call it Mount Taylor," Joey says calmly, eyes still closed.

I blink at him in the rearview, which, of course, he can't see. I blink many times.

Stay positive. Stay positive. Rational explanation incoming.

I wait. All I hear is the air cranking. Finally, I break.

"Mount Taylor? Are you serious?"

Grant sighs. "Yes, Dad."

"Just want to be sure we're talking about the same Mount Taylor here because the Mount Taylor I think of when someone says 'Mount Taylor' is the one west of Albuquerque, which is, oh, a little over a hundred miles away."

"That's the one," Caroline says, lifting her face off the vent and flopping back in her seat.

"Okay," I say, nodding to myself. "So is this a good time to ask *why* we're making a cannonball run to Mount Taylor?"

Caroline looks back at Grant, and Grant looks over at Joey. Joey takes a deep breath.

"Because we're in a race against the wind," Joey says.

He lets it go at that.

"Right," I say. "A race against the wind. Naturally."

I look back at the headlights in the rear. They don't seem to be gaining. With any luck, Hos warped an axle running up that mountain face, and we might stay ahead of him, at least for a little while. I glance at the gas gauge.

"Grant, what would you guess this thing gets per gallon?"

He doesn't skip a beat. "About twenty on the highway. I made a few adjustments to get her there." He opens his eyes and leans forward. "I swear I topped her off just a few days ago."

"Well, she's not topped off now. Half a tank isn't going to get us to Mount Taylor."

"There's a station at Crownpoint then nothing much till you hit I-40," Grant says.

Driving anywhere with anything less than three quarters of a tank of gas goes against my very being, but the high beams of Hosteen's truck look like they've receded a little bit more. If we're making any headway against them, I'd just as soon keep going.

"We could stop at Crownpoint, make it quick," Caroline says. Running out of gas is one of her deep-seated fears as well. We were meant for each other.

"We'd be talking F1-style quick," I say. "And if we're not and Hosteen rams the pumps, the night gets a whole lot hotter."

She frowns and chews at her thumbnail. The way she crosses her legs and bobs her foot tells me she has to pee too.

"I get it, but if we press on, maybe something changes. Maybe he needs gas too. If this gets twenty a gallon, highway, then that monstrosity he's driving has to top out in the tens. I mean, you saw it."

Caroline turns around. "Joey? What do you think?"

That kind of stings. I'm trying to be decisive here and give her a plan or at least show her I can still make plans. Plus, foresight was never really Joey's strong suit. He's a great guy—don't get me wrong—but he's the man who robbed hospitals for drugs so that he could stay alive while phasing well past what anyone in the Circle would call safe. He did it all for a good reason, but still.

Joey hasn't opened his eyes. He breathes deeply. Maybe he's asleep. I wouldn't put it past him.

"He doesn't seem too concerned," I say after a minute.

"We can deal with the gas when the gas becomes a problem," Joey says, proving my point in a perfectly Navajo way.

"We can't phase out of this if things get hard," Caroline says softly, threading her fingers over her stomach, and again, I get the sense that she's holding something from us, that she's hurt somehow or knows something that maybe her sight showed her. But for whatever reason, she doesn't want to share it. I try very hard to convince myself that Joey or Grant is the one she doesn't want to speak plainly in front of, but self-doubt has been creeping around my brain more and more these days. I can't help but think I'm the one she's not being straight with. Maybe she senses what I sense, that I'm fraying by the day, right along with my collars. Maybe the ten-year itch finally caught her. I hear you can have those even when you're not technically married. Maybe my son has a ten-year itch too. Maybe the itch is me. *Am I the itch?*

Either way, we pass the Crownpoint Quik-N-Go in silence. It doesn't even look open, which, come to think of it, makes a lot of sense. It's four in the morning. Officially, twenty-five hundred people live in Crownpoint, but I've been to the health facility here on rotation, and I would say that number is very generous. I doubt anything here could support a twenty-four-hour establishment. So we were going back and forth about the gas, worrying about nothing.

Navigating the patchy concrete here is tricky, and I have to slow down more than I like. We lost Hosteen's headlights at the turn, but I know he's back there somewhere.

We pass darkened double-wides, one after the other, the truck-in-and-drop kind that the Navajo Nation provides. Wheelchair ramps snake absurdly back and forth across the fronts of many, painted bright red. I wonder if those come standard with the drop these days.

I press on the gas, and the tires thwap softly as they run over a patchwork of packed dirt and worn concrete until the sound becomes a soft hum. I ease back in the seat with a wince—the long-haul lower-back pain is creeping in earlier and earlier these days —and try to focus on the road ahead. But not checking the rearview every ten seconds is hard. We're on a straight path to I-40 then Mount Taylor beyond, but I keep feeling like we're just waiting to be overrun.

THE GAS LIGHT ticks on when we're about five miles outside Thoreau. Everyone sees it light up. Grant swears. He used to owe me a buck for that, but I do believe this warrants it.

I know this stretch of I-40 better than anyone really should. I've driven it hundreds of times on rotation from ABQ General to the Chaco Health Clinic back in the day, when I was just a simple doctor trying to deal with one realm of reality. It's a bleak stretch of road.

"There's nothing past Thoreau until you get down by Bluewater," I say flatly. "If we're thinking about gassing up, this is it."

The back of the truck is quiet.

We hit a straightaway that gives us a decent view of the road ahead, going black to purple in the creeping light of the early morning. We're in the trust lands now, a checkerboard of valleys and plateaus that look a bit like they could've been mountains once but then someone took a knife to the clay and gave them all the same flattop haircut. The land was deeded by alternating sections, so drivers flit in and out of Navajo jurisdiction. Caroline stretches and looks behind us. She sees what I've been seeing. A few headlights are staggered in the near distance, but nothing resembles Hosteen's light array.

"Gas is now or never," I say.

Caroline looks at me and nods. Grant does too. Joey is still asleep.

That's what I've been waiting for. Family quorum. *Pit stop it is.*

The exit takes us off trust land. I remember a big chain gas station just before the highway here, awkwardly shiny and clean, coming from the Rez world. I see the halogens before I see the station, lighting up the sky like a parked UFO—the good old Speedy Mart.

Six pumps gleam. Lights in the store windows blink advertisements for the holy trinity of all highway fill-ups: beer, cigarettes, and the lotto.

I rap my thumbs on the steering wheel as we turn in. "Alright. I'm on gas. Caroline, you run in and pee like you've never peed before. Grant, Joey, watch our butts."

I pull in hot and park us with a jolt. Caroline throws open her door and runs toward the mart part, where a quick glance shows a very bored-looking teenager behind the counter.

I watch the purple distance and swipe my card in and out of the reader well past when it says Processing. "C'mon, c'mon."

I get approved just as Caroline is handed the bathroom key on what looks like a foot-long monkey wrench. She disappears into the back as I accidentally hit Premium. The light goes green—no time to reload the gas. Premium it is. You're welcome, truck.

I stick the pump nozzle in and click it to max fill then cross my arms and turn to watch the road from whence we came.

The gas keeps filling and filling. I look at my watch as though any of this has anything to do with the seconds that tick into minutes that tick into hours on this earth—force of habit.

"Sure is a thirsty car, Grant," I say, trying to keep things light.

Grant looks up at me with a look that says he didn't hear. I drum my fingers on the hood with woodpecker speed.

Lights crest the hill, and my heart skips a beat. But it's just some old sedan with bouncy shocks, yellowed with age. They pass us by.

Finally, the gas clicks off. I pop it out and vigorously screw on the gas cap before sliding the pump into the holster, then I'm back around and in the driver's side and buckled in, waiting for Caroline.

"How long can it take her to pee? For crying out loud." I laugh nervously.

We've been here for five minutes, which is four minutes too long. I get whiplash looking back and forth from the road to the store, store to road, road to store.

Caroline appears from the back, distastefully holding the wrench key in one outstretched hand.

"There was no soap," I say to the quiet crowd in the rear cab. "She hates it when there's no soap."

I think maybe we're actually going to get out of here with enough gas to get us to the mountain, then I turn back toward the road.

Something that looks a bit like a black boulder rolls into view in the distance.

"Shit," I say.

The black boulder opens up its engine.

Joey's eyes open in an instant, and he leans forward.

Hosteen's truck is eating up the road between the hill and the Speedy Mart. Without the light bar, without the blazing double set of headlights, the truck somehow seems even more obscene, a roaring shadow moving far too quickly. And it's on a collision course with my family.

15

CAROLINE ADAMS

I'm not a huge fan of gas station bathrooms. I don't know anyone who is, except maybe truckers or anyone else where the alternative is a hole in the ground, but I really do not want to pee in Grant's truck, and I don't think the boys want that either, so we all agree that I have precisely four minutes to run in, hit the powder room, and run out. *Speedy Mart, speedy pee.*

The problem is, of course, that when I get inside the Speedy Mart, I have to spend at least thirty seconds rousing the cashier, who looks incredibly stoned, so that he can find the bathroom key.

"Around here somewhere," he says, rummaging in a sticky-looking drawer.

I force myself to stop tapping my heel like I'm in a dance recital. "Do you really need to lock the bathroom out here? What's the concern?"

He looks up at me drolly. "You'd be surprised," he says and hands over a grubby wrench, which I take without further comment.

The gas station bathroom looks about like one would expect a gas station bathroom under the stewardship of an incredibly stoned teenager to look at five in the morning. I spend way too long considering where the most hygienic place would be to put the grubby key before settling on the top of the basin.

I proceed to do the hover.

Some might assume that being a floor nurse would accustom me to germs, but in reality, the opposite is true. It's accustomed me to a lifetime of disdain for germs and an overwhelming feeling of disappointment at the many, many people in this world who don't do the super-easy bare minimum to keep them at bay.

My hover pee done, I chance the soap dispenser and am totally unsurprised to find it empty. Then I give everything up for lost, flush the toilet *with my hand* and open the door *with my hand*, which ought to emphasize how seriously I take the Speedy Pee Directive.

I'm walking back up to the register, wondering if I have time to buy a little bottle of hand sanitizer, wondering if this place even *has* hand sanitizer, but when I get to the register, my droll friend is staring out the window with a quizzical look on his stoned face. I follow his slack gaze and find the boys getting out of the truck one by one: first Joey, then Grant, then Owen, who looks back at me with wide eyes and pushes his hand out in a motion that seems to mean "stay there."

Very soon, I see why. Hosteen Bodrey's truck is on a collision course with the gas station. He drove up on us in dark mode.

"Shut off the pumps," I say.

That's a thing, right? I know you can shut them off

outside. Mom calls those things the idiot buttons. If they can be shut off outside, they can be shut off inside.

The kid just keeps looking out the window.

"Hey! You!" I snap my fingers a few times and get his attention. "Shut off the pumps, or that truck is gonna blow us all to Santa Fe!"

He's startled back to the present and absurdly checks his pockets before locating the general shutoff in the back by an ancient-looking phone. He flips the cover up and presses the button. Something clicks. I hope that's enough.

"Get down. Stay low," I say. Then I walk out the door.

Owen wanted me to *stay there*.

Yeah, right. In what world would I sit here and watch all of them get blown to pieces at a gas station? Where Owen goes, I go. For the record, I really hope that doesn't mean getting blown to pieces, but the way Hosteen's truck is gaining momentum, things aren't looking great.

Outside, the truck's engine sounds like some angry giant sucking a milkshake. Owen yells for Joey's help. He nods and does what he does, which is surgical phasing. He's gone in a blink, and a second later, a scuffle breaks out in the front of Hosteen's cab. The tires shimmy shake, and the truck brakes hard, fishtailing on the broken concrete. All sorts of stuff is going on inside, but the glare of the gas station lights on the windshield makes it hard to see.

The truck stutters again, accelerates, then slams into the outer pump maybe fifteen feet from where we parked.

The pump pops with the sound of a tree snapping in half. Glass shatters. I cover my face and feel something glance off my cheek, which goes numb. I'm feeling for blood when someone grabs my hand. Owen looks quickly at my face then pulls me aside, along the wall of the gas station, out into the early-morning air. I take a few deep breaths. I once had a nurse manager who I hated, but she did give me one decent piece of advice: if you can't do anything, at least take deep breaths. So that's what I do.

I was hoping the crack came from the truck, but it looks like it came from the pump. The grill of Hosteen's truck is mashed up, and one headlight hangs like a loose eye, but it seems to have dealt a lot more damage than it took. And now it's backing up. It moves like a zombie— lurching, braking, lurching—but it moves. The pump line wraps itself around one toothy tire until it goes taut then pops off in a spray of gas. More gas comes out, and more. Then it stops. *Cheers to you, master idiot button.*

Grant's voice sounds tinny and distant in my ears. "He should be out by now."

He's right. Last time, Joey jumped in, turned the truck, and jumped out. It's been too long.

The truck shakes from the inside, and someone cries out inside. After a quick look my way, Owen moves forward. Grant follows, one hand on his shoulder, father and son. Their smoke rolls over one another. It's family smoke. I can't help but look down at my tummy, hoping. But if something's there, I can't see it.

Before they can get to the truck, the door pops open, and Hosteen and Kai jump down, first one, then the other, with Joey Flatwood between them.

I don't need to see his smoke to tell something's wrong. He's stunned, jammed up. He stumbles to the ground, and they pull him standing again. He doesn't even seem to see us. His eyes are an off-planet kind of distant.

That creepy white smoke streams from the eyes of the Bodreys now just like it did from Dark Sky. In a way, it *is* Dark Sky. His power is here, a hundred miles from the trading post, and when Hosteen speaks, I feel like Dark Sky is speaking.

"The Diné have regained a true warrior today. Joseph Flatwood will be honored in the world to come."

Little tendrils of the white smoke that snakes from their eyes have found their way into Joey's. Bigger tendrils are questing, crawling up his chest, cupping his cheek.

Joey yanks back and forth like a bull in a chute, but only for a moment, before his knees buckle and both Bodreys have to strain to hold him upright again.

Some part of him is still here, but I doubt it will be for long.

"Let him go, Hos!" Grant yells, his voice strong and clear. "Whatever you're doing, we want no part of it."

"You have no part in it," Kai says with such finality that I can almost hear the way it slaps Grant across the face. "You will open the way, and then you will be left behind."

"I don't understand," Grant says, the hurt pushing his voice high. "Kai, you were applying to college a few weeks ago. You were gonna rent a little apartment in ABQ. I was gonna visit you every weekend. We had..." When he trails off, a lump forms in my throat. "We had so much to look forward to."

Kai blinks the smoke clear from her eyes for a heart-beat, but in a flash, they're milky white again. Grant couldn't have seen it, but I did.

"Remember who you're talking to," I tell Grant. "This isn't the girl you know."

"Yes!" says Hos. "Remember who you're talking to. The first people. The people who have broken through three worlds to land here. And who will break through three more if that's what it takes until we find our *true* home."

Joey is shaking his head like he's stuck in a bad dream. His strong, red smoke is changing, drying out, flaking. In its place is this brilliant, burning whiteness that loops from eye to eye to eye across all three of them.

"You're hurting him," I say. "I know you can see that. He doesn't want whatever you're doing."

Kai's quiet answer chills me. "He does. He just doesn't know it yet."

Owen shifts in that subtle way I know means he's going to do something brave and reckless. It's what got him that first bullet wound in the shoulder. He was brave and reckless for me. He reaches into his pocket for his crow.

"Owen, wait—"

In a flash, he's at Hosteen's throat with the broadside of his forearm. It's a solid connection, but Hos barely flinches. The smoke seems to have his back, keeping him standing. And when he grabs Owen with his free hand, the smoke pours over Owen too. He may not be able to see it, but he sure looks like he can feel it. He yanks free again and rubs at his arm with a sick grimace on his face.

Grant starts to walk forward. This, of course, is exactly what they want, what Hosteen wants, what Dark Sky wants. They eye his chest with dripping hunger. But Grant doesn't see that. He sees his friend being toyed with by a thug who's been a pain in his ass since the day he set foot on the reservation. Part of me thinks Grant would trade the bell and everything else for one solid uppercut, a knuckle-to-jaw connection. I wouldn't blame him.

But he can't. And he would know that if his brain hadn't gone all thirteen on him again.

My fingers twitch with the need to do something, anything, and that's when I hear the soft rattle of the bathroom key.

I'm still holding the toilet wrench.

My legs make the decision before my mind can catch up, which, to be honest, is actually a good thing because I sometimes think my brain is still somewhere in my twenties. My body, though, has been living for a long time in this unyielding high and dry desert. And it's holding a foot-long monkey wrench.

I sprint past Grant's slow-menace walk and swing low, sweet chariot, right for Hosteen's knee. He may have some help from Dark Sky and the smoke, but so far as I can tell the toilet wrench doesn't give a damn about that.

Hos falls to the ground, howling, and as I stand over him, twenty-four-year-old nurse Caroline pipes in from some deep recess of my brain: *That patella is no longer where a patella should be, and you made it that way.* Then Owen holds on to me like I'm the lifeline he needs, and all that imposter syndrome nonsense flits away. In its place is anger, righteous anger.

I help Owen stand and run a hand lightly down his forearm. Where I pass, the burning white recedes, and his ocean-blue smoke returns in small shoots. Joey staggers to the ground, and Grant moves in to get him, but I don't want him getting close. Hos seems more interested in his wonky knee at the moment, but Kai still has that awful, open hunger. Without her brother as backup, the burning white tendrils search for a new place to root, and she's still gripping Joey's arm with an unnatural strength.

"Kai, honey, let go."

Kai looks back and forth between me, Hos, and Grant. Her breathing quickens.

"I love you because my son loves you. But so help me, God, I will hit you in that beautiful face of yours with this wrench if you do not let go. And just so we're clear, this wrench has been in that gross bathroom, getting poo fumes on it for probably *years*, Kai. And it's gonna get all over your face."

She looks at me strangely, and I know I probably went on too long, but this is my first assault with a deadly weapon, and I'm all crazy with adrenaline and something else—something mama bear.

Kai lets go. She backs away, looking at us like *we're* the animals.

"Walk inside, Kai," I say.

She does, slowly, with that weird silence back upon her. The white smoke seems stunned for the moment.

She opens the door to the Speedy Mart, me right behind. The little ding strikes me as so ridiculous that I have to press the back of a hand to my mouth to keep from laughing. I'm trembling like a leaf. Adrenaline is pumping and dumping. I wonder if Kai knows she could probably scare me to death with a strong *boo.*

The stoned clerk watches us with eyes like dinner plates. "Is this really happening?" he asks.

It is, buddy. Welcome to the club.

I point inside the very soap-free women's restroom. "Get in."

As she does, I unclip the grungy old carabiner to free the bathroom key from its prison.

I poke my head in. "I know it may not seem like it at this precise moment, Kai, but I'm still really rooting for you and Grant." Then I close the door, lock it with the key, and axe chop the key with the wrench until it bends, bends, then snaps off.

I slide the toilet wrench over the counter to the clerk on my way out. He bobbles the catch, and I hear it clatter to the floor as the doors snap open in front of me.

I pause. Back up. "Also, there's no soap in the ladies' room. Just FYI."

16

THE WALKER

art of me follows my friends in their desperate flight to the Turquoise Mountain. Part of me is already there. But the part of me most present is still standing in the swirling smoke and ash and sand of Dark Sky's Windway gone wrong.

Chaco snatched the black bear totem, which seems like it was important for Dark Sky to initiate others into his fan club of white-eyed fanatics. He has a solid group of them—almost fifty by now—I can tell because of the way their threads are tugging strangely at the great rope on which I walk. They all yearn to go to the Turquoise Mountain, but not in a good way, not in a pilgrimage way, like Gam. These souls are more like sleepwalkers bumping up against a closed door again and again.

We all stand in the eye of the storm—well, not Dark Sky. He's sitting, humming deeply to himself and fashioning something out of wet ash and black clay that looks disturbingly like a new bear totem. This guy is relentless.

A good chunk of the crowd that gathered here have understandably decided they want to bail. This wasn't the

Windway they signed up for. But Dark Sky isn't letting them. A handful of these people of Chaco—my people—try to pass through the vortex penning them in, only to get buffeted back by the spinning grit, sandblasted and bleeding from a thousand tiny cuts.

None of them try for long. Already, I see tendrils of white questing from those he's turned to those he's trapped. Soon, everyone in the eye of this storm will be turned. It'll look like one big spiderweb of white smoke unless I can figure out some way to stop it.

I swipe reflexively at the questing smoke as it passes near me, but my hand doesn't stir anything, not even a puff. It's a product of the thin place then, closer to the land of the living than the realm of the dead. I can't help but feel a flash of disappointment. I should've learned my lesson by now. But hope has a crazy way of hanging on well past all reason, so I try swatting at the smoke for a while.

Time stretches inside my mind. I'm called to a thousand places at once. Death after death, I escort each, speaking when spoken to, but I can't recall any one conversation in particular. I was never great with names when I was alive. As a cop, I got introduced to a lot of people every day, and eventually, I had to write every one of them on my pad, or I'd lose them in a blink. More and more, that's what my job feels like, white spaces in the film reel of my brain. Gone in a blink.

I come back around again and find I'm still swatting at smoke.

"Chaco?" I call out, then I feel stupid again. Chaco burned up.

"We can deal with that later," he said, his not-so-subtle way of telling me I'm losing my mind.

So much for later.

When I focus on the fact that he's gone, I feel so trapped that I get sick to my stomach. The only creature I've ever known that can communicate with Ben the Bubble Boy on his sad little floating island in time and space has just burned up like flash paper in the night sky. Judging by the lightening in east, that probably happened hours ago. I've been swatting at spirit smoke like some dumb cat ever since, not dealing with it. A memory of my mother twists my gut: before we healed the veil, back when she was in a bit of a downward spiral, they would wheel her out to that observation room, and she would try to grab on to the rainbows cast by the sunlight hitting the crystals of the dream catchers hung all over.

I have a terrible moment when I cannot remember if I've walked my mother through the veil or not. I wonder if Sitsi Dejooli is still alive.

Yes. Yes, she is. She's at Green Mesa, back in the wheelchair again, but not like before. She is aging well, almost at the end but not there yet.

My relief is a palpable thing, a cool wave that focuses me. I forgot Mom's birthday once and never forgave myself. I'm not sure what I would do if I walked her across the veil without knowing it. *Yikes.*

C'mon, Ben. Caroline and company are fighting to do their part. Time for you to do yours. Get as many Ws as you can: who, what, when, where, why, just like you did back on the beat.

As best I can, I walk back the experience of sitting shotgun in Gam's head. The white blooms of mold are already tinging the edges of this memory, too, but the picture is still clear enough. There were red flags where my old cop instincts kicked in and I got that feeling that some part or other of the story was important, something I really needed to hold on to.

First off, the Turquoise Mountain was the *where*. It was then, and it is now. One of the four holy mountains that anchor the Dinétah is breaking down again. Gam patched it up then, and we have to do it again now. Thankfully, Chaco got that across to my compadres in the land of the living before—

Well, he got it across. *Good ol' Chaco.*

Chaco's feather is key although I'm not sure how. He did not drop feathers lightly. Plus, it's threaded through generations—a gift from the bird to the elder twins, who then gave it to Gam for protection. For years, it's been with Joey, hanging around his neck.

The big blank is the *why.*

Cops can skip the why if they get the who and the how. Especially if they're members of a notoriously under-manned tribal police department with a jurisdiction of thirty thousand square miles and a pile of cases growing thicker by the day. The why is all too often a nice-to-have. Sometimes, in a world gone crazy, it doesn't exist at all.

I walk over to where Dark Sky is sitting cross-legged, eyes closed, singing in a low rumble as the wind whips around us. I can speak anything now and understand anything, but this is old speech. I catch something about asking for guidance or maybe offering guidance. I plop down in front of him, cross my legs, cross my arms, cock my head, and just watch. "Who are you, really?"

He shows no acknowledgment, nothing like Coyote. To me, this seems a very human reaction, which is to say no reaction at all. Hell, if not for the whipping wind and the creepy smoking eyes, he looks like a picture-perfect example of a Navajo elder. He's got the breechcloth, the painted face, the totem, everything dusted in pollen and ash. You could paint his picture along the outer brick of the visitors' center, right there next to the other chiefs and warriors—where the tourists like to snap selfies with their brand-new turquoise bracelets, on their way to Wapati casino.

Something catches my rambling train of thought like a root underfoot. *Look to the Story of the People.* Tsosi said that to Gam. The elder twins were always talking about the Diné Bahane', the creation story. It was one of their go-to campfire yarns, practically required listening for any young Navajo that grew up around the Arroyo and many who didn't. *Feeling lost, no direction in life? Look to the Story of the People. Need help with your love life? Look to the Story of the People. Money trouble? Look to the Story of the People. Gut problems? Look to the Story of the People.* It was sort of a running gag, tongue in cheek.

I must have heard the story a dozen times—they had voices for all the parts and everything—but my memory is still dusty. Also, I spent way too much time whispering with Joey in the back row about which of the girls were moving up and down our list to impress, as though any of them cared how far we could throw our idiot selves off a cliff into the snow.

Normally, I would just give it up for lost, like so many other memories—mine and those I escort—but I can't accept failure this time.

The twins perform the key stories every year on New Year's Eve. The Arroyo always draws a questionable crowd that night—kids set on partying and ruckus—so in the interest of keeping people out of trouble, the elder twins started the storytelling tradition.

The more I think on it, the clearer the memories of

those nights become, like I'm running my hands over the grooves in my brain where they live, scraping off the dirt, flaking away the mold, exposing what's beneath.

In a nutshell, the Diné Bahane' is the story of how the Navajo came to be where we are right now. I don't mean the Rez. I'm talking about the Dinétah, the homeland, the space between the holy mountains. Those who hold to the story believe we arrived here at the end of a long journey through a bunch of other worlds. The one we're on right now is only the most recent—some say the fifth. Our creation story, like most, has a couple of different versions. I remember it even changed a bit depending on which elder twin was sitting front and center by the fire, but it always followed the same pattern.

I'm not great with specifics these days, but I remember the gist. Each world we had to go through to get here taught us a lesson. The first world was dark. Sometimes it was an island. Sometimes it was underground. But as a kid, I always remember thinking it was gross. Tsosi was the one that would go through all the things that were there, like he was reading roll call at camp, most of them bugs. I can hear his voice now, humming through the pine popping in the firepit. *Red ants lived there. Dragonflies lived there. Hard beetles lived there. Coyote-dung beetles lived there. Bats made their homes there. Locusts made their homes there.*

Then at the end of this cosmic roll call, he would stand tall—or as tall as he was able—and say, *These people weren't like you and me. We call them the Nilchi Diné.* And then, when that didn't land on any of us young punks more interested in playing grab ass than learning our people's history, he would roll his eyes and say, *The bila-gaana name is* Air Spirit people.

The worlds in which I live go wavy for a second.

I peer at Jacob Dark Sky and wrack my brain for anything else in the Diné Bahane' about the Air Spirit People. As I remember it, they were a bit of a pain in the ass, always fighting with one another, always doing weird shit like having sex with people they shouldn't. A lesson was in there somewhere, but I don't think that's important right now. Right now, I have this image in my head of a storm of insects battering the lights of the old Quik-N-Go downtown, thrashing against each other, looking for a place to land that won't fry them.

The Air Spirit people fled the first world. Up and up they flew, led by the strongest among them until they broke through to the second world.

Dark Sky's song is on repeat—the same words as before, about a guide. But now, they've got a different color. Behind me, the smoke flits like a string of moths from person to person. It's settling in their hair and on their noses and ears, leaving little trails of dust across their slack faces. It probes like the antennae of an ant.

The Air Spirit people—and here, in front of me, is the strongest among them. You could call him a chief. He's not looking for a guide. He is the guide, just like Wind was in the time before. Hell, he could be ol' Nilch'I himself. I see the whorls everywhere, painted in ash on the people he's "saved"—the sign of the wind.

Maybe I've stumbled across the why after all.

Dark Sky wants to bring his people through to the next world, just like his ancient ancestors did.

THE PART of me back at the trading post has had some sort of breakthrough about Jacob Dark Sky that slots right into my collective memory, but this version of me is walking the rope of the living toward the Turquoise Mountain. I'm already almost there.

I used to check on Caroline's thread all the time—Grant's and Owen's too. I stopped because seeing the life they were building with each other was too painful. I could watch but never be a part of that life on the Rez, so I stopped. Then somewhere along the line, I started to lose myself.

I can't believe it's been so long since I've walked among them. Maybe cold turkey was a bad approach.

Their threads are moving, changing, weaving in and out of one another, the light within them pulsing at different intervals. The song of their lives is changing even as I walk the map. They've already run into some problems of their own, but these are things I can't do anything about. Taking this much of my mind off the day job is already splitting me thin. If I don't focus on where I'm going, my mind starts to fuzz over again.

I tell myself that once we seal off this damn wind, I'll be able to collect my thoughts like I used to without having them blown away every time I'm not looking. And I almost believe it. I would believe it, maybe, if not for the way Chaco said, *We'll deal with that later.*

So I walk on, leaving the squad to their journey, even though turning away hurts. It helps that they have Joey. *Good ol' Joey.* He was always a better Navajo than me, anyway, maybe even a better brother too—to Ana, I mean. I was all fired up right after she disappeared, so I signed up with the NNPD like I might make a difference, but then life happened. I started trying to help my family move past it. I thought I was doing the tough stuff, trying to move on. He was the one in the real shit. He never stopped looking. Even getting banished couldn't stop him.

I step out of the soul map at the base of Turquoise Mountain just as the sun breaks over the horizon on what looks like a stunner of a summer morning. Anyone just waking up here, perhaps someone who set up camp on the east side on the low slope—the approach Gam probably took—would think they scored a perfect bluebird day for a hike. The stillness of the place might seem a little odd, no birds calling, no creatures rustling the brush.

If they could see what I see, the stillness might make more sense. Beyond the veil of the living, in the thin place, a dark wind rages, ripping through the sepia, carving a path that's easy to see, down the mountain.

Gam's string has long since been tucked away into the great rope in the sky, so I can't rewind the specifics of her life to see exactly what the hell I gotta do here to shut down that wind. I guess I'm gonna have to get creative.

Some places have memories, too, just like the souls that walk them. Some places—especially places of power like the Turquoise Mountain—have a mark on the soul map as well. Even standing here, I get hints of the past that unfolded around me.

If I can backtrack the threads of the dead, maybe I can also backtrack the memories of this place.

I find the Turquoise Mountain in my mind's eye, the way it's presented on the map, as a sort of imprint passed over by millions of souls in its time. It's like a tracing a child might make by rubbing charcoal over a paper with a leaf underneath. The more I focus on the land around me, the more clearly the picture emerges.

I see a volcano, long and low with a huge cone of barren rock. Swaths of aspen trees run down the hills, broken here and there by thickets of smaller evergreens and long stretches of flat rock. Textures layer over one another until a clear picture emerges of the mountain as the volcano it was, standing tall and alone, apart even from the high desert that surrounds it.

I fix myself to this place on the soul map and hit reverse, which is like looking at a time-lapse where the world moves around the camera but the focus never changes. The Turquoise Mountain—Mount Taylor to the rest of the world—stands like a sentry, unmoving through the seasons. The runs of aspen trees go from leaf to bud to barren, then their yellow leaves jump back up, and the face of the mountain explodes in autumn gold. The seasons melt away. I go faster. The sun reverses its way overhead. The stars shift in the sky, reframing everything. I could keep going and going, back before the white settlers, back before the Navajo. I bet I could go all the way back to when the first souls found themselves here. The picture would be far less defined, with far fewer souls to walk this place, but I could do it.

That sounds kinda nice, actually. I could just binge-watch humanity in rewind, going from today's seething mishmash of souls figuring out ever more creative ways to claw over one another, watching as they wink out, back into the becoming.

Hell, even if I took the picture back a measly hundred years, the world would have maybe a third of the souls I wade through every day. How much more rested I would be if I cut the number of deaths in half. I'd have so much more *me* time. Whoever did my job back then had no idea how easy they had it.

My laughter scares me.

Before I get lost again, I take my hand off the map.

Focus, Ben.

I'm here to find out how Gam sealed the broken anchor at Knifepoint, not to get lost flipping through the sands of time like a maniac, wishing things could be different.

You get what you get, Chaco would say. *And you work with it.*

I need a frame of reference to get the year right. The easiest way for me to picture time these days is still "Ana time" and "After Ana time." Gam's memory—the one I hitchhiked—was right at the turning of the page. Ana was still alive when I was doing stupid teenage cliff jumps, but she wouldn't be for much longer. She died the following spring.

I whip time away, peeling each year off like the layer of an onion, until I reach that dark year. The Turquoise Mountain looks the same. Sometimes, people think their grief is so powerful it can move mountains. But one of the terrible and wonderful things about life—a thing I only really noticed once I was no longer living—is that the soul map always stays lit. The rope I walk goes on. Your life can fall apart, but the mountains stay standing in the after just as they did in the before. And it's for the better.

I'm more careful now, peeling back the months then the days like parchment paper until Gam appears.

She's stepping out of a cab at the trailhead in big-banded snow boots and a stately buffalo-check jacket that goes down past her knees. She arranges a thick scarf of her own design around her head and face, situates her buckskin purse, and pays the driver a chunk of cash. He looks like he has a bit of Navajo in him and seems to understand when she says she'll pay him extra to hang around.

"I'll be nearby. You're not the first Diné I've driven to Tsoodził," he says in Navajo before pulling away.

"Well, how about that," I say aloud.

I was wondering how she got here, especially without me or anyone else in the family knowing. She never drove. I don't even think she had a license. But there you go. She probably took the transit bus off the Rez as far as she could go and caught a cab the rest of the way. I bet she even knew the cabbie. I'm not sure what I expected, maybe for her to arrive on horseback or something.

Snow falls lightly on the empty gravel lot at the trailhead. Not a lot of hikers come in the dead of winter, I guess. The mountain usually has an incredible vista view, but not today. Today, it's gray all around. The sky feels close. Fat white flakes fall in little swirls, with no wind to speak of—not, at least, in the living world.

The thin place is another matter. It looks then the way it looks now. And even though Gam can't see the way the dark wind rips through this place, I know she senses it, probably can even feel some of it through the bell around her neck. The wind is drawn to the bell, just like every spirit thing I've come across in this world and the next.

I hear a skittering sound and turn to find Chaco—sorry, Blackfeather—landing awkwardly in the lot. The full force of the spirit wind may miss Gam, but it's certainly hitting Blackfeather. He looks like some sort of glitch in the map as he does his awkward two-step bird hop over to Gam. Pinned low, he blinks furiously against a force nobody else can fully see or feel. His feathers ruffle wildly. He's jostled this way and that, like an old car in high winds.

Seeing him is wonderful, and it breaks my heart all over again.

Eventually, the dark wind proves too strong, and Gam has to go over and pick him up. She cradles him at her core like a big black cat.

"This could be harder than we think," Blackfeather says, looking up at her pointedly. His voice comes through to me in this soul sketch just as it did when he and I spoke.

Gam just nods. A sun-scorched wooden sign standing like a lonely sentinel in the flat desert off the lot reads Gooseberry Trail. They set off that way. Past the canyon walls, it starts to climb quickly.

Gam steps confidently along the ridgeback, holding her bundled bird. More than once, she turns her head my way, and each time, my breath catches for just a brief second before I remember this is a reel from the past. She's just getting her bearings, remembering the time her mother—my great grandmother—took her here.

The trail hooks around a jutting column in the red rock of the canyon wall, and here she stops for the first time. She's breathing hard, but not, I think, from physical exertion. This is spirit work.

The canyon rises steeply above her, sheer and clean-cut, and here she is sheltered from the sparse snow, but the dark wind roars. Every step she takes toward Knifepoint seems to strengthen it by a degree.

"It is that way," she says, pointing off the path, down a trail that looks barely used, covered in brush and loose rubble. Blackfeather follows her gaze then looks warily up at her.

"Are you sure about this? No shame in returning to the twins, asking for help from the Circle."

The shake of her head is both minute and final. I know that shake well.

"I am the only one that can knit the anchor true again," she says. "And time is short."

Blackfeather presses himself closer to her and says nothing, only digging his head into a fold in her jacket.

She follows the trail from memory, and her memory is good. The dark wind blares. I can see the trail we're meant to take as clearly as if a herd of elk trampled it just ahead of us, but in the physical realm, it's barely noticeable. We're far off anything on a trail map. As we weave our way through a thin field of boulders, Gam stops again. At first, I think she's faltering, but as she leans against the damp face of one large stone, she looks down at her bundle of bird, and the concern is written plainly on her face.

Seeing why isn't hard. Blackfeather doesn't look too hot.

"What's wrong?" she asks him.

"Nothing. We must hurry."

Gam hears the strain in his voice as clearly as I do. She takes her forefinger and brushes gently along his downy ridge, and it comes away black, as if she dipped her finger in ink. She looks at it and pinches her mouth, holding it for him to see.

"Just molting, that's all," he says.

Gam rubs her forefinger and thumb, and the black is blown away in the unseen wind. She gently shifts Blackfeather to the crook of her other arm and takes stock of herself. The red checks of her buffalo plaid are streaked with black as well.

"You're coming apart," she says.

Blackfeather is silent.

"I know when you're hiding something from me," she says, genuine concern in her voice.

After a moment, Blackfeather says, "I am a thinning.

This place is a thin place. The wind seeks to break through here. So it also seeks to break through me." The blunt Navajo logic of his words reminds me so much of my grandmother that I wonder if perhaps more than a little bit of Blackfeather's mannerisms rubbed off on her. Or perhaps it was the other way around.

Gam sucks at her teeth. "And it is succeeding," she says.

More of a statement than a question, but Blackfeather bows his head anyway.

"We need the Walker," Gam says, and even though I know she's talking about the guy who had the job way back when, before me and before Ana, the simmering anger in her voice hits me too.

"We do not have the Walker," Blackfeather replies, and his disappointment hits just as hard.

This guy must've been a real gem—stepped out for cigarettes and never came back, abandoned them.

Or he forgot them.

In the back of my mind, I can hear the last conversation I had with Chaco echo like distant thunder down a canyon.

"I don't think I'm all right... in the head."

A terrible realization surfaces in my brain, rising like a blood moon. If the Walker can help fix the spirit wind, maybe it's because the Walker caused it in the first place.

"Go, then," Gam tells Blackfeather. "Leave this place."

Little bits of black dust stream from his folded wings. "I will not. My place is with you. Until the end."

Gam mutters a Navajo curse but gently, and as she walks on, her eyes glisten.

They pass through the field of boulders in silence and head toward what looks like a sheer stone face. Chaco is disappearing more by the moment. I have a wild urge to skip forward to the part where she makes all this right, or maybe even past that so that we're all back in the lot at the trailhead, waiting for the cabbie, where I imagine the two of them saying, *That was a damn close thing. Let's not ever do that again.*

But something stops me. Something doesn't quite track. My cop-fu is raising a red flag in what should otherwise be a pretty straightforward account of how to fix this mess.

Just as the two of them look like they're about to walk into a wall of stone, Gam steps to one side and disappears. For a second, I think she's gone, and I stand there blinking stupidly. Not until I'm quite literally an arm's length away do I see where she went. The banding of the rock face disguises a gap with eerie perfection.

Inside is a rough-hewn set of a dozen or so stairs that look like they were offered up by the mountain itself. The blank gray sky shines through at the top.

Knifepoint is up there.

Gam and Blackfeather are about halfway up but slowing considerably. The wind cuts through both of them. Blackfeather is a shade of himself, disappearing like a Polaroid developing in reverse.

I hear another sound too, one so strange that I pick it up clearly under the wind, probably because I've never heard it before.

Gam is crying.

It's not unlike her singing, to be honest, just quieter.

She leans heavily against the rock wall. "I cannot do this, Blackfeather."

"You must," he says. "When I am gone, there will be nothing between you and the wind but the bell. It can protect you for a short time, but soon, the wind will take it. And it could be lost to your people forever."

"It is so… heavy," she says, hunching herself, but carefully, as if Blackfeather might crumble entirely if she hugged him fully.

She keeps climbing. And now, she is crying in song.

It's a song I know.

A hundred memories flick through my mind, rapid fire, like an old-school slide projector: Gam sitting in her chair inside her spartan room, rocking and quietly knitting while she hums the tune I'm hearing now. Gam between Ana and me on the couch, knitting, singing the same song. Gam at Ana's bedside at the hospital, her distaste for the place plain on her face but still knitting and humming and singing, sometimes dropping words in the place of tones, her nose a soft whistle while the needles click in time.

The song is "Shí Naashá." It's not a song about knitting at all but one about going home.

Ana asked her once what the lyrics meant. I wanted to know, too, but by then, she'd sung it a thousand times over a hundred different scarfs or blankets or shawls, and I guess I figured I'd missed the boat to ask. Like I said, I'm not the best Navajo. But Ana had the fire inside.

Gam said "Shí Naashá" was a song to celebrate when the white man released our people from internment at Fort Sumter. Once Ana knew the lyrics, she sang it all the time in Navajo and English. I can hear her now, running back and forth along the only clear path from the front of our duplex to the back, her little feet shushing along the carpet then slapping over the linoleum then out the back to shush through the grass again, singing as she went.

I am going in freedom.
I am going, I am going,
I am going in beauty.
I am going, I am going,
I am going. Beauty is all around me.

Gam sings it in Navajo only, of course, and even watching as I am, a ghost in a memory, I can still sense the power those words have here, the connection. We were released from a prison, and from that prison, we found a home. We sang that song until we found the Dinétah anchored here, at Tsoodził, Turquoise Mountain, one of four.

Blackfeather cannot speak any longer, but he bobs his shadowy wisp of a head in time with Gam's words. I feel like some sort of creep, walking around them, looking down from on high as Gam's tears pass through Blackfeather. Behind me, the stairway plateaus at a flat mesa, and the blank gray sky casts everything in a hollow light as if the entire substance of the memory is being drained right alongside Blackfeather.

"How the hell did you get out of this one, Gam?" I ask her, yelling now over the roar of the dark wind. I'm yelling so that I can hear my own voice and assure myself that I'm still here, looking back, that this is a memory.

At the top of the steps, Gam takes the full force of the spirit wind. She's hunched over her chest, and I know the weight of the bell is almost too much.

She looks down at her cradled bird, barely there. Blackfeather says nothing. I don't think he can speak any more.

Gam looks past me, through me, to where the mesa rolls over itself like a wave of rock. There, at the tip of the overhang, where the roll should meet the flat, is a gap, a vortex of spinning white about as long a buck knife, where reality is missing.

Knifepoint.

My first thought is *It's way too big to sing closed.* I was expecting a few cracks, maybe a splinter fanning out across the stone, something Gam could pile some sand or clay over and pat down, sing and seal, and that would be that. But knitting this closed is more like trying to stitch up the exit wound of a .45.

Gam tries again anyway. She shoves herself up with her free hand and stumbles out into the open mesa. She's trying to make a run, grasping the feather necklace now, pressing on, and Blackfeather is blown away.

He's blown totally away. None of this is adding up. None of this is how I thought it was supposed to be.

She cries out in anguish in a way that so closely mirrors the way Grant cried when he saw Chaco's final flight that my vision wavers and timelines get crossed in my mind.

Gam takes one look at the break, her teeth gritted, her gaze razor-sharp.

Then she turns around and runs after the dust of Blackfeather.

At the stairwell, she manages to capture a handful of dust but no more. Still, she nods in victory and pulls her hand inside her jacket.

She starts singing again, the "Shí Naashá," her knitting song, and walks quickly down the rock stairs. With each step, the palmful of Blackfeather's ashes thickens.

"Hey!" I yell. "Gam, what are you doing? You close it up! You're supposed to knit it shut!"

I can't help it. I was always the type of guy that talked

to the TV. The more things change, the more they stay the same.

She ignores me, of course, walking with more conviction, the wind at her back. Her jacket swells above the bell, where her palmful of Blackfeather's ashes takes the rough shape of a thing again, then a football-shaped thing, then a football-shaped thing with a beak.

By the time we're on the far side of the field of boulders, Blackfeather's wings are back, gossamer black in the dead light. By the time Gam crests the first of the ridges back down to the trailhead, he's poked his head out of her jacket at a break in the buttons.

"What are you doing, Naba?" Blackfeather asks, sounding as astonished as I am—perhaps more so since he was basically air before Gam knit him back together again.

I bet that was quite the trip.

"I cannot do it," Gam says.

"But—"

"But nothing, my bird," she says.

Suddenly, I know where I got that snap that brooks no argument. I only bust it out when I have to, but when I do, the souls that screw around get the message real quick.

"If I thought your sacrifice would seal the break, I would have made it," she says. "But the tear is too big. The wind is too strong. Without the Walker's help, you would be destroyed for nothing and the bell lost forever."

In the lot once more, Blackfeather slowly steps onto her shoulder. He grips her tightly since the dark wind is still strong, but it's nothing like the force of undoing it possessed at Knifepoint, at its source.

"Then we are lost," he says. "The Walker cannot be reached. The anchor will fall, and so will the Dinétah, and then the wind will spread far and wide until the entirety of the living world becomes just another thin place where no life can exist for long."

Gam stares back toward Knifepoint with a warrior's look, the kind of look that says the fight is far from over. "There is another way," she says, "a sure way."

Blackfeather looks closely at her. "You cannot mean to ask—"

"I must think," Gam says. "Signal my ride," she says. After a moment, she adds, "Please."

Blackfeather takes a few staggering steps and spreads his wings. Whatever this other way is, he knows it as well as Gam, and the thought of it seems to hit him like a body blow. He looks back, uncertain.

"Everything comes again," she says, nodding encouragement as he pumps his newly knitted wings into the sky and takes off to find that very understanding cabbie.

"You didn't make it," I say to her, still dazed. "You couldn't knit it closed."

But she did close it eventually. We know that.

And judging by the way Gam sits in the dirt, cross-legged, her head in her hands, wracked with silent sobs, whatever she does to seal the deal comes at a terrible price.

17

GRANT ROMER

I hear phantom sounds of Chaco everywhere. The truck mirrors cuttin' the wind as we roll down the highway sound like the way his wings sliced the air when he was about to land on my shoulder. The mesh-net tie-down in the bed flutters just like his wingbeats. I listen as hard as I can with my head and my heart for his voice, but that part of me has stopped working. It ain't just quiet. It's gone.

Joey places a hand on my knee to try to comfort me, but the guy looks wrecked himself, like he's just trying to hold on for dear life after whatever Hos and Kai did to him in that truck. Some things even Mom can't heal up all the way.

"You ready to talk?" I ask him.

"I was about to ask you the same thing," he says, head back, eyes closed.

So not yet, then. The four of us sit in silence, and I pretend not to notice the way Dad checks on me in the rearview mirror every couple of minutes. He was never really good at silence.

"Why don't we talk about how your mother kneecapped Hosteen Bodrey with a monkey wrench?" Dad says.

I try to smother the smile, but a smile sometimes don't want to be smothered.

"That was pretty awesome, Mom."

Joey nods. "Badass."

Mom wipes her hands on her jeans and looks out the window. "I didn't *want* to do it. But the wrench was there, and so was his knee, and then one thing led to another, and suddenly, he's on the ground and I'm locking Kai in a gross bathroom." She turns around, and I can see she's conflicted. Part of her is proud, while part of her is horrified.

I don't know nothin' about mothers. Mine died so long ago that I got more memories at her gravestone than I do in her arms. But I bet Mom was all-in on Kai, just like I was, expecting a future that took years to build together but only an instant for the wind to rip apart.

She grips the headrest and reaches for my hand. "Honey, I'm so sorry about Kai. I don't think I really could have gone through with... kneecapping... her too. I don't want you to think I'm a violent mom or anything."

I stop her right there with a squeeze. "It's okay, Mom. You did what you had to do. Did a lot more than I did to get us out of there and keep the train movin'."

"You would have wrenched her, Caroline," Joey says flatly. "If you had to."

Mom slowly turns around and stares out the window at the sunrise. Soon, we'll be driving right into it. A new day has begun, but I've never been so tired.

"What about you?" Joey asks, opening his eyes and looking over at me, head still rested back.

For a split second, I'm afraid I'll see the same strange whiteness there that I saw in Kai, but his eyes are still dark brown, almost black, and as clear as a winter night.

"What about me?" I ask.

"Are you going to do what you have to do, if it comes to it, with Kai?"

"What's that supposed to mean?" I ask, feeling defensive.

Joey just watches me.

But I'm about done with that. "She's in there, man. She's in there because she has to be in there. You want me to talk? Fine."

All of a sudden, I'm talking about Chaco, and I have no idea where it's coming from. It just bubbles up. "I know y'all think maybe he's gonna come back. He's come back before. He's magic. Not really alive, so he can't really die. But let me tell you this: he is gone. He's gone like any other thin place can disappear. Like the mountain is disappearing. He's gone because when *everything* is thin, then *nothing* is thin. And I already lost one chunk of my heart today, and I'm about done losing chunks of my heart. So she's in there. She's gotta be."

I'm not sure when my eyes got all misty or where the hell this lump came from that bobbles like a chunk of ice above my Adam's apple. I clear my throat and lean back. Mom squeezes my knee but leaves it at that, and that's enough.

I focus out the window for a while. Dad slows at the Grants exit and follows signs for 547 North. I hear more phantom Chaco, this time a little ticking sound that mimics his talons when he walks on the shingles of the roof above my bed in the A-frame.

Walked. When he walked there. He ain't walking anywhere no more. Or flyin'.

That ticking sound, though, it ain't going away. And Dad notices it too. He slows down, and the tick slows down. He speeds up, and the tick speeds up.

He mutters a curse and shakes his head in that what-the-hell-else-can-go-wrong way of his, which I always thought was a bit of a dangerous challenge to the weird world we live in.

"There's somethin' in the tire," I say.

"She's been pulling a little left for a few miles," Dad says. "I think we've got a flat."

Caroline looks at him then back at us and through the window behind. We're all thinking the same thing and have been for miles. Locking Kai in a bathroom ain't gonna stop her for long. And even a wrench to the knee ain't gonna stop Hos. Normal Hos would walk the rest of the way on that busted knee if he had it in his mind to try and kick my ass. And this Dark Sky Hos has a weird fire in him. Wherever they are, they ain't far behind.

"Do you have a spare, Grant?"

"'Course I got a spare."

Dad takes one more long look out the rearview mirror. A fair number of cars are on 547 now. We're solidly into normal people's morning time, where they do normal things like go to the office in ABQ or sit down for a nice breakfast.

"Alright, I'm pulling over. Otherwise, we'll be coasting to Mount Taylor on rims."

Dad eyes a stretch with a wide shoulder and flips on the hazards, slowing fast to stop.

I unbuckle and thwap Joey in the chest to bring him back from zoning out again. "C'mon. Everybody out."

Soon, all of us are on the side of the highway with trucks careening by. Dad and Mom are looking back up the road like they'd be able to give us any real notice, and Joey looks like he's zoning again.

"Hey, Flatwood," I say, bringin' him round. "I'll change the tire if you tell me what's going on. What did they do to you?"

This time, Joey nods. Mom and Dad gather in as I grab the tire iron and slide underneath the bed to free up the spare. Full size, of course—people who ride on a doughnut in our stretch of the country ain't gettin' very far.

"I saw what they saw. In Dark Sky. In the vision he has. And..."

He swallows hard, like he wants to push the words back down.

"And I get it. It makes sense in a terrible way."

I slip off the bolt I'm trying to loosen. "Don't tell me you're on board too."

"No, my friend. Don't worry. I'm just saying I wish it made no sense. I wish he was just some witch or agent of chaos like before. But if he was, he'd never have so many Diné on his side. His power is strong, but if Kai and Hosteen and all the others wanted to break it, they could. That is why he is dangerous. Some part of them *wants* what he has to offer."

"What on earth is he offering?" Mom asks as I pull down the spare along with a whole mess of road dust.

When I slide back out from under the bed, Joey is struggling to explain. I want to keep him talking, but I also want this tire on and us out of here before we get into another situation. As far as I know, Mom left that wrench back at the Speedy Mart.

"What do you know about the Diné Bahane'?" he asks after a moment.

"The Diné what?" Dad asks.

He looks at Mom, who shrugs. Both look at me.

"It's the creation story," I say, grabbing the jack from the toolbox in the bed. "How everything came about—First Man, First Woman, the worlds, all that."

I remember reading a thick black book about it back in high school as part of the mandatory language and culture classes. It was long, and a lot of it was lost on me. I've been pretty well introduced to Navajo culture over the years but more in the dropped-into-the-boiling-pot way. I've learned enough to know I'll always be an outsider, no matter what Kai used to say. I see that now.

Joey gestures out at the big sky beyond this ugly stretch of road. "We had to go through four worlds to get to the one we live in now. Our oldest ancestors, First Man and First Woman, they only came about in the fourth world. Before them, there were the Air Spirit people."

I lay the tire flat and feel blindly for the jack fit under the frame. A gust of hot wind skitters trash down the highway. I run my tongue along my teeth and spit. Mom allows it without comment, which is rare.

For a second, we all look back down the highway, watching, waiting. Then the jack clicks into place, and I start pumping it up.

"I remember I wasn't a huge fan of them," I say.

"They weren't like us. In the story, they're described as insects—beetles, dragonflies, ants. Things that travel in the air and fly swiftly like the wind."

The wind is picking up again. I have to squint to focus on loosening the lug nuts. I'm not sure yet if Joey is saying what I think he's saying. But if he is, we may be in deeper than I thought.

Dad clears his throat, his hands in his pockets, jingling my keys nervously. "Does it say anywhere in there how to deal with contagious hysteria, by chance? The kind that's probably driving ninety miles an hour down the highway right toward us on a cracked axle?"

Joey bobs his head back and forth, actually considering. But he doesn't take the bait. "The Air Spirit people were... troublesome. They fought with each other, couldn't keep it in their pants, offended the tribes. They got kicked out of the First World pretty quick. The Second World too. They were lost, trying to find a home and bumping into the sky."

I swap the tires and place the lug nuts, spinning each with my hand and trying not to think of the hail-like sound the locusts make slamming against the halogens of the Quik-N-Go. *Was it always that bad? Or did more come along with the dark wind?*

"But each time they got lost, they found a guide. The one that told them how to get to the Third World was Nilch'I, the Wind. He peered down from the sky and pointed the way. It's said he has a white face and his words are the breath of new life."

"Dark Sky," says Mom. "His eyes. The smoke that obeys his words."

Dad puts his hands on his hips and looks at us all like we're crazy. "You're telling me that Jacob Dark Sky is the Wind?"

Joey bobs his head again in that yes-and-no way. "I'm telling you that Kai and Hosteen believe he speaks with the power of the Wind."

I tighten each bolt until the metal squeaks, one after

another. My hands suddenly feel very slow. "But I thought Wind was a good guy, breath of life and all that."

"Good and bad are hard to come by in the Diné Bahane'. Things have many sides, especially the Holy People and the powerful spirits. But the first time Wind comes on the scene, it is as a guide for the lost Air Spirit people."

I yank up on the tire iron one last time then pop it back into the truck bed. The jack squeaks as it compresses, and the truck settles again. I think back to that crazy Windway ceremony, the way the people there seemed in step, gathering strength from the songs, like they were being prepped for a journey. I remember the snakes and the storm and the swirls of ash, all symbols of power for the wind.

"Sounds like Dark Sky to me," I say.

"He has joined others too. Kai and Hosteen showed me. Most of the Diné at the ceremony are his now, which means most of the Arroyo." He grimaces at the memory and shakes his head as if to clear it as I chuck the jack into the bed along with the flat and slam the gate closed.

All of us get in, four quick slams in succession as Dad fires up the engine. I wipe my brow and take the jug of water again and listen to the suck of the engine as we pull back out at speed.

Mom turns to watch out the back window. "So far, so good," she says.

But I'm uneasy. The way she glances at me, I know she can read it on my face, and it's probably written in my smoke as well. A different kind of wind is gathering. It runs at a crosscurrent from the hot gusts blowing trash down the highway, almost like two shifting plates. It tugs at the bell, adding a tiny bit of weight with each mile that rolls under the tires.

"Maybe the wrench put them out of commission," Dad says, managing a very awkward-looking smile.

"They're coming," Joey says. "Dark Sky is guiding them."

"Where?" Mom asks. "To us?"

Joey leans his head back again and closes his eyes. "No. Through us. And out. To the next world."

I look up at the bluing sky. Picturing it as thin as a robin's eggshell is all too easy. The idea of worlds beyond worlds ain't foreign to me at all. I got the key to ours hanging around my neck.

"When the time is right, you will give it to me."

The longer I wear the bell, the more it feels like a noose.

"I understand why they want to go," Joey says.

He leans forward and stares at the floor of the truck, through the floor, really. Maybe he senses the strange new wind too. "After what you've seen on the Rez, can you blame them?"

When he finds Dad's eyes in the rearview, Dad is the one to look away. I know what they're thinking. I've been all over the Rez, in and out of the schools. There's poor, then there's Rez poor. Kids go without shoes, without food. Others are sick from booze and drugs. No jobs, no money—there's just this great *lack*. And that ain't even saying anything about what Mom and Dad gotta see day in and day out, what Ben Dejooli saw in the NNPD— record overdoses, exposure, people dying in remote huts from things that one pill can take care of just a hundred miles away in ABQ.

"The bilagaana tried to wipe us out years ago," Joey

says, as if plucking my thoughts from the air around my head. "First with war and then by the long, slow theft of our lands and our people. They failed. But sometimes, it seems like we ourselves are picking up where they left off."

The San Mateo mountain range has been coming together out of the morning haze for the past handful of miles. Now, Mount Taylor is as clear as day. It doesn't rise out of the range so much as center it, anchoring it. And, if we're right, it anchors a whole lot more.

"Doesn't seem right," I say. "To just up and leave like that. Jump worlds. Even if it does sometimes suck here."

Joey leans back again and closes his eyes. "The Diné are supposed to be here. In this world. Even if Dark Sky can guide us through, it's not right for us to leave. I feel it, but I don't know why. And if I don't know myself, I can't tell Kai and Hosteen or those that follow."

I see his point. *How do you tell a people who are hurting to go back and maintain? That it's their lot in life to suffer? Pay no attention to the man behind the curtain, who offers a new world. Go back about your business.*

That is what the Smoker would call some primo white-people-shit way of thinkin'.

"Can he do it?" Dad asks, breaking the soft whine of the truck cutting the wind. "Dark Sky. Can he...?" Dad shakes his head, seeming to have trouble even allowing the possibility. "Can he open the way and take them through?"

Nobody seems to have an answer for that. I sure don't. All I know is I don't want to live in a world where there ain't Diné.

"I don't think we can chance it," Mom says.

That about sums it up. She puts a hand over Dad's on

the console and runs her finger over his bracelet. He's worn that old bead bracelet as long as I've known him. A Diné girl gave it to him when he fixed her thyroid at the CHC and changed her life. I know the Rez takes a lot out of him but only because he's willing to give it. The Rez means as much to him as it does to me. Maybe more.

He hits the gas and gets us back to speed. Mount Taylor looms front and center, bigger and bigger by the mile.

18

CAROLINE ADAMS

I guess maybe I'm expecting Mount Taylor to look like an iceberg crumbling into the ocean with all this talk of dark wind ripping it apart, but it looks like any other mountain to me. In fact, the view looks a lot like what I see every day in Navajo country, just bigger and sort of piled all together in a hump.

Then again, I'm not exactly what you'd call a mountain person. I'll refer back to Exhibit A, my Keds. And no, I don't have any hiking shoes back at the A-frame either. Just more flats.

We've parked at the trailhead lot, and everyone's stretching outside the pickup, working the kinks out, Joey in particular. My guess is he doesn't travel by car often. He's more of a crow guy. Owen's dress shirt is damp at the back. He's spinning his bracelet and trying not to look lost. A flush of gratitude—of love—hits me hard. Here's a man who lives most of his life on the left side of his brain, throwing himself in the deep end of weird again for us, for me.

For a second on that last stretch of highway, I thought

I was getting nauseous and that maybe it was morning sickness, and I was happy. Can you believe that? I was happy at the thought for just a flash, until the rational downer side of my brain listed all the real reasons I might be nauseous. Chief among them was that I haven't eaten a real meal in twenty-four hours, and I've essentially been running on a strong cocktail of anxiety and adrenaline.

But that flash was there before I stamped it out. I know what I felt. And what I felt was happy.

The funny thing is that downer Caroline, who buried that happy flash in dumb logic, might want this pregnancy to be viable more than anything. She wants it so much that she's afraid to allow herself to believe because she won't survive being crushed if it doesn't happen.

Yes, I realize I sound crazy—literally talking-to-multiple-personalities crazy. But I've had a hard couple of days. I'm hoping once we get back to the A-frame and I can sit on my couch and eat a big bowl of pasta, I'll be able to get it together and really look for smoke coming from that nest way down inside. Owen's already caught me staring awkwardly at my tummy a few times on this trip.

I'm not sure why I don't just tell him except that I don't want him crushed either. I would rather take the crushing myself, both downer Caroline and I, than see it in his eyes. I know how much he wants this.

"Can you feel that?" Joey asks, tapping the leather pouch slung low next to the feather around his neck.

"The crows are colder," Owen says. "Responding to the mountain, maybe?"

Grant itches at his chest, where the bell makes a small bump, barely noticeable. But I know it's heavier than it looks.

"So where do we go?" Owen asks. "This is a pretty big mountain."

Joey grips his crow and phases out for a second with a *whoosh pop* that echoes like the crack of a rifle through the empty lot and against the sheer stone cliffs around us. The area is strangely quiet—no birds overhead, no rustling in the brush. Even the desert bugs seem like they're waiting.

Joey pops back, startling all three of us. He points at a wooden sign in the distance that reads Gooseberry Trail. "The dark wind flows from this direction. If we go against the flow, we will find Knifepoint."

For a second, we all just sort of stand there. Times like these, the first step is always the toughest, especially when you have a literal mountain to climb. The best thing to do is just take it.

The dark wind we walk against doesn't press back on our bodies, but I can see it press back on our smoke. Grant has the most drag. He's holding on to the bell over his shirt like it weighs ten pounds, and try as he might, he can't keep the grimace off his face for long.

We zig and zag with the trail, hugging the rock face for a bit before hitting a fork out in the open. The way we take looks like nothing but a squirrel path, but the smoke says otherwise. The dark wind is strong here. My totem pouch feels like a block of ice against my leg. Even Joey holds his off his chest.

The squirrel path opens to a flat stretch on the far side of a ridge, where a bunch of big boulders are scattered. Grant bumps from rock to rock, his smoke streaming from him in little jets of glittery cinnamon. Joey's smoke evaporates from his shoulders like mist scorched by the sun, but he still helps Grant forward.

Owen and I are no better. He's a few steps ahead of

me, but his bright-blue smoke sifts down and all over me. I try to grab it, to rub it into my arms and shoulders as if I could save it, but a person's smoke is theirs alone. Once it's gone, it's gone.

The boys' smoke has always been consistent, but my color has always been all over the place. Just like my mind, it shifts and moves on the daily. It's always low-key annoyed me that I can never seem to pick one color to commit to. Right now, I'm purple, and I have no idea what that means. It's just dumb purple all over except this weird little bit here at my tummy that flickers the soft yellow of a candle flame.

I stop dead in my tracks and slap both hands over my mouth, but I'm not quick enough to keep the gasp in. The boys turn back toward me.

I hear Owen ask if I'm okay, but I can't stop watching the little flame. It's the most beautiful thing I've ever seen, and I'm crying because I see how fragile it is, how it sputters. It wants to grow bigger, but the dark wind tugs at it too. I cup my hands over it again and again, but it does nothing to stop the sputtering.

Owen walks over and rests a hand gently on my shoulder. I look up at him through bleary eyes, and I can see the understanding physically come to him. It's more wonderful than I could have hoped. It's like a bookmark thunked between the pages of his life, creating a very clear *before*. What comes next is the *after*.

"I think... I think I've got something here," I say lamely. "Something very good. But it's so small, Owen. And this place, the thin place—it's no place for a life that could be."

He looks me up and down like I'm some sort of medical miracle, which we are. Although until now, I've never really understood why. Then he just hugs me, hard at first. He lets up like he thinks I'll crack something down there, which is hilarious coming from a medical professional that should know it doesn't work like that. Only one thing can really snuff this out right now, and it's me fighting the dark wind all the way to whatever awaits us at Knifepoint.

"So that's why you wouldn't phase," he says, smiling adorably, like some teenager after his first kiss. Then he walks me back a few paces, quickly. "Go. Away from here. We'll be fine. Get back to the car. Hell, get back to the Rez. Or if that's not far enough, just keep driving. I'll find you wherever you go."

I laugh and wipe my eyes as Joey and Grant reach us. "I think the lot at the trailhead is okay for now," I say.

"What's going on?" Grant asks.

Owen clears his throat. "Your mother... uh, well, you see, your mother and I..."

"I'm pregnant," I say.

Grant's the first to pick his jaw up off the desert floor. "When you wouldn't phase, I thought you were... well, like, sick or somethin'. This is *way* better."

"But it's not a sure thing," I add. "And I have to get out of the wind."

Grant joins Owen in shuffling me off. "Then go! Go, go!"

"You don't know what's up there, Grant. Be careful. All of you."

Owen flashes me that old smile, the one that says *I got this*, and I honestly don't think he could have mustered it even a minute ago. Joey unwinds his black feather fetish from his totem pouch and hands it to me. "For protection," he says.

"I can't take that, Joey. That was Gam's gift to you."

"And now, it's my gift to you. And you," he adds, sweeping it over my core and holding it out again. "Take it. Please."

Before I can protest again, he puts it in my hands. The little turquoise stone it's lashed to gives it a sure weight, a good weight. The feather feels smooth and sharp. "Thank you," I say.

I realize none of them are going to start climbing until they see me going down, but walking away is harder than it sounds. I love the smoke of my boys as much as I love the smoke of this new thing. But in the end, those three can protect each other. I'm all this little thing has.

I start down, holding the feather over my tummy. It helps, even if nowhere but in my mind.

19

OWEN BENNET

Being terrified, elated, and in a moderate amount of pain all at once is a new feeling for me. I'm used to feeling emotions one at a time. I assay the field and pick the feeling that suits it. If the problem is medical, the emotion that suits it is *focused concern* in diagnosis then *relentless drive* to ameliorate the issue. If the problem is relational, the emotions tend to range. Sometimes, empathy is called for. Sometimes companionship. Sometimes passion. If I've screwed up—and believe me, I have, many times, both with Caroline and with Grant over the years—it's usually because I've dialed in on the wrong emotion for the wrong time. I approach Caroline with empathy when she wants passion. I approach Grant with companionship when he's looking for empathy. I grew up in a household that led me to believe that if you simply pick the proper emotion for the time at hand, you win the game.

If my dad was still alive, I'd love to sit down over a glass of bourbon and ask him just what the hell I'm supposed to do when every emotion hits at once.

Caroline is pregnant. I love her, and she's pregnant. I'm dog tired, in over my head, a little lost, and I want to pop a bottle of champagne. Plus, I'm weirdly aroused, maybe at the thought of my gonads actually working. All this while we're in a desperate race not to lose what little foothold the Navajo people have left in this world.

And now the dark wind we're following has run us right up against the flat wall of the canyon.

None of it makes any sense.

Joey grabs his crow and pops out then back a few seconds later. "It's strange. I see the wind but not the path."

Grant sits down in the dirt. Joey follows his lead. Both look beaten down. On top of his carrying the bell, I know Grant is terrified he's going to lose Kai forever, if he hasn't already. I know Joey holds the weight of all the tragedies that hit the Dejooli family on his own shoulders, along with everything else, including the fate of the Arroyo.

And I know another thing too: I know Jacob Dark Sky is a thief. Doesn't matter if he's actually Navajo or not. In fact, it's worse if what he says is true and he is Navajo, because the only thing more reprehensible than a thief is a thief who steals from his own people. I still don't think I'm entirely wrong when I cite collective hysteria. It's just that Dark Sky stirred it all up. Kai, Hosteen, and all the others in the Bodrey camp are not acting under their own power. They're operating under his.

I square up to the cliff face and reroll my sleeves. I'm not about to turn around and go back to my pregnant life partner and say, *Sorry, honey. Got stuck at a wall.* I know what she'd say. She'd say the same thing she says when I can't find the mustard in the refrigerator: *"Did you really look?"*

Grant and Joey look like they could sleep here for a week, but I start pacing. Back and forth. Back and forth. I stare at the cliff that will not beat me. And that's when I see it. When I swing far enough right, the banded rock shifts on me a bit.

I step up to the shifty spot and reach for the rock. My arm passes right through—a subtle trick of the mountain, probably older than time. Behind the break are rough-hewn steps.

"Up we go, boys," I say, sounding a lot like my dad. "All we needed was a change in perspective."

Grant musters himself to standing like he's been called in for a day shift after a long night on the floor. Joey cracks his neck and rolls his shoulders, careful with his crow. The totems are so cold that they're hot.

The stairs lead up to a hidden mesa, open on one end to the joyless blue sky. Mount Taylor rolls over itself on the other side, like a frozen wave of rock, very nearly touching the mesa again.

It should be touching the mesa. I feel it. Know it, some-how. It's as if that wave completes the blood flow of the mountain itself. Without it, the venous structure of the land is stinted, blocked. I can see it as clearly as if I was looking at a coronary angiography and seeing bright nothing where veins should be.

I also see Kai and Hosteen Bodrey on either side of that bright nothing.

Kai is sickeningly mesmerized by the blurry white space between, crouched down like a child staring too closely at the burning fuse of a firework. Hosteen is bobbing back and forth as he stands, ready for something, anything. Both look our way as soon as we top the stairs, no triumph in their eyes. Nothing is in their eyes but a mirror of that white void.

They beat us.

I'm not entirely surprised. I am utterly dismayed, but I'm not entirely surprised. Something Joey said in the car rings in my brain: *"Things that fly swiftly like the wind."*

Maybe the whole world has gone crazy. Maybe Kai and Hosteen really do have a touch of the Air Spirit people to them, and we're watching the Navajo Creation Story act two, writ large. Or maybe they just know a faster back road and didn't blow a tire along the way. Either way, they got the drop on us.

Grant groans when he sees them and pushes himself away, back against the rough rock wall in the barrel of the wave. He clutches his chest and grits his teeth like he's having a cardiac episode. The bell is pulled toward this void, and Grant's heart is tied to the bell. So in a way, that makes sense.

I feel a pull, too, but toward the ground, like during the Windway. I try to go to my son, but the dusty rock underfoot seems suddenly made of molasses, as if the hollow gaze of the Bodreys is miring Joey and me. I know it's that wicked smoke Caroline sees. The stuff that leaks from their eyes is pinning us.

Well, if I can't walk in the land of the living, I'll walk all over them in the thin place. I reach for my crow totem and only dimly hear Joey's cry of warning.

Too late.

The thin place is a terror. The unseen wind is very seen here, and it broadsides me with the force of a real wave, the kind that sucks you under then spins and pins you to the bottom of the ocean floor. No water here—only white creeper vines falling from the eyes of the Bodreys and spreading like varicose veins over the sepia fabric of this place. It's a spinning whirlwind of madness and infection, and I want nothing to do with it.

I let go of my crow, but my crow won't let go of me. The tendrils have closed over me, over my hands, over my legs. I can't walk, am barely able to see through the whipping smoke.

I'm trapped here, where the white void blazes with blinding strength. And the cold burn is already beginning.

20

CAROLINE ADAMS

I'm sitting on the open bed of the pickup, legs dangling in the air, my hands cradling the crow feather over my flicker. The feather actually does help. I think it exists on a couple of different planes. The flicker has superfine dust, a new soft yellow color that's also somehow bright, like the fuzz of a baby chick, and while it slips right through my fingers, the feather seems to help keep it together. I keep thinking of the way waiters cup their hands over that complimentary plop of ice cream with the candle at a restaurant on someone's birthday, and how it almost always goes out on the way to the table, and they have to relight it. But I don't think this little one could be relit. If it goes out, I think it's out.

I've been watching this little thing for as long as it's been here, so I see very clearly when the dark wind shifts and the push becomes a pull. The downy dust of the flicker is slowly plucked, strand by strand, back up the mountain.

Something happened at Knifepoint. What was pushing us away is now trying to suck us in.

"Don't go, little one," I whisper, threading the feather gently between my fingers. "I'm just getting to know you."

I shouldn't be here. Even this empty parking lot at the trailhead is too close to whatever weirdness is happening at that anchor. When the flicker starts to fade so that even the feather has trouble catching its light, my mind is made up.

I hop off the truck bed and slam it shut. After a few seconds of rooting around on the driver's side, I find the keys pressed between the visor and the roof. I'll just go back to the main road, maybe head to the nearest town and get a coffee. *Wait, not a coffee. Maybe a water or whatever pregnant women drink. Juice?* Anyway, the wind won't be as strong there.

Yet. The wind won't be as strong there yet. If we can't nail down this anchor point again, the world is going to get very windy very soon.

I set that thought aside. *First things first.* Box number one on my life list is "Keep flicker flickering." I fire up the engine and check the rearview.

And I see a beat-up old truck coming up to the trailhead lot and, behind it, a bus that looks like it's limping in on its last legs. A rusted-out RV is behind that, then a few more trucks, and on and on down the line—a Rez caravan, but one that looks more like a funeral procession. They pull in, park, and kill their engines one after another. The lot isn't big enough for all of them, but that doesn't seem to matter. Cars start stacking up along the shoulder, just like they did back at the Bodrey trading post.

I sink into the seat and try to disappear, watching out of the corner of my eye as every single person that emerges from these cars walks to the entrance of Gooseberry Trail like it was their own backyard. Their smoke is being sucked from them in great gouts by the vacuum at Knifepoint, and I'm not surprised to see that it's that same bleached white. The color says something was there, but now, it's not anymore. Dark Sky took it. Now, he's got a hundred or so soul canvases primed to paint any way he likes.

They walk quietly and speak little. I wish I could say they look like zombies—brainwashed, absent—but there's nothing aimless about them. These people are alert, alive with drive and purpose. I recognize many of them, and I know that's saying something.

There goes Johona Nez, pregnant at sixteen and a type-two diabetic. I've been chasing her down for weeks to watch her $a1c$ levels, for the baby if for nobody else, but the Nez family lives ten deep in a double-wide in a place on the Rez they call the Boxes, and she has her hands full.

Shilah Yazzie walks by, helping his father, both of them on oxygen. They're lifelong smokers with CPD pressing down on their chests, adding stones by the year. They still smoke, even with the oxygen. Shilah's brother got drunk two years ago and fell asleep with a cigarette in his hand in their trailer, but Shilah forgot to seal the O_2 right, and his brother blew himself to pieces. Everyone thought it was another meth cook gone wrong until Shilah came to Sani Yokana, the police chief, sobbing, and told him the truth to clear their name.

Others walk by, and even though I have a hard time following the instructions on the back of a box of mac-n-cheese, I remember almost every name. They're Navajo from many different clans, but the common thread is that they're miserable, suffering, desperate. And they think Dark Sky can set them free.

Kai's mom, Bly Bodrey, is being helped along by two of the Bodrey cousins, her ankles so purpled and swollen that she can barely lift them. I'm not sure how she plans to get all the way up there, but I believe the tendrils of white smoke will help her along. Dark Sky won't leave any behind.

My heart breaks at seeing the Smoker walk by, eyes forward, face set. He carries his pack on his back and has a cigarette tucked behind each ear. Maybe the smoking finally caught up with him, and he woke up in the middle of the night, coughing blood. Or maybe he was tired of hocking his cures on a card table by a gas station, barely earning enough to eat the crappy Quik-N-Go burritos. In any case, he obviously has more faith in Dark Sky than in the future he sees for himself on the Rez.

I understand a bit of the pain Joey felt when the Bodrey kids showed him as much. *Who the hell do we think we are to tell these people they can't leave?* They don't know what waits on the other side of Knifepoint. Nobody does, except maybe Dark Sky, but if there's one shot in a hundred that it's better than the mess they live in day in and day out, maybe it's their right to take it.

How am I supposed to tell Shilah Yazzie—a man so mistrustful of the white man's medical system that he won't use an inhaler that could give him another five years if he just did as prescribed—that Dark Sky may not be who he says he is? *Even worse, if I did, would he care?* Fall is coming soon, then winter. And winter is hard here for sick people living hand-to-mouth with nothing between their homes and the cold desert air but a couple inches of sheet metal or the thin fabric of a tent.

And there, right on cue, is Dark Sky himself, the center of the web, literally. His smoke ensnares all around him even as the whole group is pulled up the mountain. The cane is gone. No hands help him along this time. He follows the path of the dark wind with confidence just short of swagger, and the people surrounding him seem not even to care that he's a blind man about to climb a mountain. Maybe they know by now that he can see in other ways that make him the navigator here.

I doubt they see that he's simply swapped one wooden cane for a hundred or so human ones.

If anyone here notices me, it will be him. For whatever reason, my second sight makes me that much more visible to people who walk between worlds. I'm a strange thing to them, like a dirty blonde in a sea of gossamer black hair. And when he sees me, he'll take me back up—and snuff my flicker out.

I know I should be freaking out, and maybe preflicker Caroline would have freaked out a little. *Okay, maybe a lot.* But I feel no panic now, only clarity.

Today has been a lot, and I just need some time with my flicker.

"Okay, little one," I whisper. "Time to get real quiet. But not too quiet. Just quiet enough that he can't see, okay?"

I take a deep breath and smooth myself out. I do everything I can to pat my own smoke into myself, like shoring up a sandcastle with wet sand. I almost lose it all when I see the little flicker doing the same, getting quiet and soft and small enough that the feather can cup the whole thing. *It listens to me! That makes me one for one! Batting a thousand, Mom!* But now's not the time to celebrate.

The minutes tick by like syrup as Dark Sky comes into

the rearview then pauses. If it's possible for a person to become a ratty old driver's seat, I do it. I hold my neck so low that it starts to cramp.

He waits, looking around as if he smells something but can't quite pinpoint it. The crowd stops around him, five, then ten, then twenty people bunched up feet from the truck bed.

I think smooth thoughts, small thoughts. I breathe very deeply and very slowly. The pull of the dark wind is still there, but I make less smoke to pull. I try to picture every part of me tucked in tight, like I'm being held by Owen, by Ben, by everyone I know and love. And I do the same for this little flicker.

And Dark Sky moves on. The crowd follows him slowly away from the lot and up Gooseberry Trail, where they thin out in a single-file line without saying a word to begin their trek.

When the last of them passes the trail marker, I get out, puffing a huge breath and shaking myself big once again. I can't be totally sure, but my flicker seems to do the same—a good sign. Inside my guts, the pendulum of my inner moral compass is swinging back again. Dark Sky and a whole mess of his new friends are on a collision course with my family, my flesh-and-blood family, and I'm down here in a truck, watching it happen.

They haven't closed the anchor yet. I don't want to admit it, but it's true. I walked all the way down, did some tailgating, and watched the Dark Sky parade, and our smoke is still getting pulled upstream, with more force than ever.

Something isn't right. The boys are in trouble.

I look down at my tummy. "What am I gonna do?"

If only my flicker knew Morse code. Oh, and I also knew Morse code.

I lean back hard against the truck and focus for a while on not crying in front of my flicker. *Another few minutes.* Another few minutes with it is all I ask.

Then another few minutes are gone, and I feel even less like wanting to risk this tiny thing. I've never seen anything like the color it has. It's my perfect color. I didn't know that, but it is. I'm amazed by how a thing could come along and nail my perfect color like that. It's magic.

But it's going out.

Before I know it, I'm crying in front of my flicker, which is a little embarrassing. And now, I'm wallowing, which is a bad thing to do when an important decision needs to be made, and just when I think I might just cry until whatever happens at Knifepoint happens, for better or for worse, my flicker is tugged by a draft.

I've felt that draft before, a few times. The first time was back at ABQ General on the day of that awful code. I was on suction, working on autopilot, running on adrenaline, even after we lost the patient and Owen called in the time of death. He and I were cleaning up afterward, and I felt the draft. It prickled the fine hairs on the back of my neck.

It means Death is stopping by.

Normally, I'd be thrilled. He's been gone so long. It's possible to miss Death, you know. That's hard to explain, but it's true.

Not this time, though. This time, I'm afraid he's on the clock.

"Hi, Ben," I say, through tears.

A song comes to me. The one Ben's grandmother sang when she said goodbye to him on that terrible day when she lay broken on the floor of her bedroom. I don't know the words, but I know the tune. Soft and sad but somehow comforting.

I brush the little flicker with the fine end of my feather and start humming my own goodbye.

21

THE WALKER

We've got a situation here. Gam never closed the anchor. And since she never closed the anchor, I can't know how to close the anchor, which means the only real family I got left walked right into a trap that I don't know how to get them out of.

So many thoughts are popping rapid-fire in my head that I can't keep them straight. And on top of all that, I've got the day job to do. The soul train never stops.

I ignore the pull of the newly departed as long as I can, staring at this soul sketch of the moments when Gam abandoned the anchor and turned away, knitting Blackfeather back together as she left, and I keep thinking, *Nah, she's gonna turn around. Any minute now.*

But she doesn't, of course. This story is already written. And worlds start to collide on me. I can't keep the picture alive any longer without her presence here, and I'm losing focus anyway because it makes no sense. *Something* happened. The wind stopped. I know that because I lived in a wind-free Rez with Gam for years after the day she turned around defeated on Mount Taylor. So somehow, the wind went away. The problem is I kind of went all-in on Gam's pilgrimage here being able to give me instructions that I might somehow be able to relay to my friends. That's a lot of *if*s, I know. And now Dark Sky has called my bluff, and I've got nothing to show for it.

I snap back to the present on the rope, back to the living reality where the pot I left simmering is now boiling over.

The Bodrey siblings beat my crew up to Knifepoint and are playing goalie at the anchor. Then Owen, being Owen, decided to try to take control of the situation and promptly got himself trapped in the thin place, where he's slowly freezing to death despite Joey's best efforts to pull him free.

Meanwhile, Grant is sucking wind, and I can see why —the bell is like a literal anchor around his neck. It's molded from the substance of that weird realm on the threshold of life and death. It wants nothing more than to disappear, and Kai and Hosteen look like they want nothing more than to help it.

Dark Sky is near too. I can sense his snake thread. He's leading his tribe, and if Grant lets the bell pull him into the thin place, the door opens, and we're done. And he's dead, which, as I'm looking at his string right now, isn't far from top of mind for him. He's in a bad place. He wants to rip the bell off, but he knows as well as I do that's not in the cards. When you sign that cosmic dotted line as Keeper, the ink sticks. Believe me, I know. The bell has to be given or taken. Otherwise, it's his burden even if it grinds him into the dirt.

He's barely holding the bell back, but he's doing it. Until, that is, Kai turns the tables on us by walking right up to the vortex herself.

Her thread, bleached bone white by Dark Sky already, starts to fray. The soul fibers it's made of snap one by one like it's caught in a tug of war.

Her hand grasps at the blinding white of the break.

"No, no, no," I say, echoing Grant and even Hosteen, who is wide-eyed.

"Moment of truth," she says, looking straight at Grant with those brittle white eyes. She may be under whatever weird thrall Dark Sky has placed upon these poor people, but that doesn't change the fact that she holds the trump card to getting the bell for Dark Sky.

Grant is in love with her. Whatever world she walks in, he'll follow. She may not be able to drag Grant to that break, but she can make him come of his own accord, and she knows it.

He starts pleading—the ugly, sobbing kind, the kind I see a lot in the moments before I escort souls through the veil, the real kind. I can barely hear his words, but that doesn't matter. He's already inching forward. It's written on his face and on his thread—if she goes through, he'll follow, and Dark Sky wins.

And here I am, worthless. I'm no more real in the thin place than I am in the living world. I'll enter stage right when the thin place kills Owen, then Grant, and then likely even Joey, who will fight to the very end to save all of them, like one of those poor souls who jump in after the drowning only to get dragged down themselves.

Then they'll see me. Then they'll see me all too clearly.

This damn job. It would kill me if I wasn't already dead. Even now, I'm getting pulled toward the day job—something strong, close, and hard to ignore, even as my people fight for their lives at Knifepoint. *And where is Caroline?*

The itch turns into a tug, refusing to be ignored. I look uselessly into the sky. Then I rip open the soul map and go where I'm called.

And there's Caroline.

For a moment, I'm so shocked that I look around to see if anyone else saw what just happened even though I know damn well nobody can.

But maybe Caroline herself did, in her own way.

"Hi, Ben," she says. And she's crying and holding the feather that Joey Flatwood is supposed to have.

That ain't good.

The feather is the only part of this puzzle that I'm sure needs to be up there at the anchor, and it's here, over her stomach.

And she's pregnant.

And in an instant, everything comes together

"Shit," I say, and I sit down on the hard ground.

"Five years, you disappear," she says, eyes on her hands, cupped over the feather, cupped over herself. "And now you decide to show up?"

She's trying to make light of it, trying and failing. And it stings because I know she's right. And I know she knows why I got called here.

"Don't take it, Ben," she says. "It's so small. It's not even a thing yet. You can't take a thing that isn't even real yet, can you?"

I hold my head in my hands, because I can and I have —many times. I am the shepherd of every death, from the ancient all the way back to the idea. Even sparks have a soul, so to speak. If it can be willed into existence, it can die. And if it can die, I get called.

"I'm sorry, Caroline," I say, and for the first time since I can't even remember, I'm crying. I probably haven't cried since, well, since the last time we had a chance at one-sided conversation together.

She goes slack, a bit like Grant did mere seconds ago at the top of this mountain, and for much the same reason. Both know they're up against a wall.

"When is it okay to stop fighting for something you love?" she asks.

She's looking for an answer I can't give. I push myself up and step over to her and cup her jaw as if I could touch her and comfort her. If she could hear me, I would say, *Never. You can never stop fighting for something you love, whether it's a place or a people or a family.*

But that would ring pretty damn hollow, coming from the one that takes it from her. And now, I look down at it for the first time and see it's putting up a hell of a fight, her little spark. It's stronger than it looks, a thread nearly formed despite having been forged in a spiritual hurricane. That makes sense, considering who its parents are.

But it's guttering, and guttering threads get the shears. It's always been that way and always will be. But I know I'll never be able to forgive myself.

My mind fogs as I form the shears over the little thing. The mold is coming back, and I see it now for what it is: a defense mechanism. It numbs me. Forgetting is easy. Remembering is what's hard. But I'd rather forget this, and as I let myself get split into a hundred pieces again, I feel the dark wind strengthen.

The break formed because of me. The dark wind is strong because of me. When I'm pulled apart—when the Walker is pulled apart—these places get pulled apart as well. As Chaco used to say, there are rules. The balance between worlds is fragile. A crack between worlds can shatter real quick if I'm not there to patch it up. Gam had to turn away all those years ago because she had no help. She needed the Walker, and he had abandoned her.

Time is a circle. Everything happens again. Chaco said that too.

Right you were, buddy, I think. For once, though, I'm glad he isn't around to see just how badly history seems to be repeating itself.

"Time to go, little one," I say. I can barely get it out.

All my timelines are crashing down on me, which is why I'm not surprised to hear Gam's knitting song, the "Shí Naashá." I would sometimes be up late at night, scared of this or that, impending adulthood then impeding death, and I would hear it from her little room, where the light would be on, each word marked by the soft click of knitting needles.

> *I am going in freedom.*
> *I am going, I am going,*
> *I am going in beauty.*
> *I am going, I am going,*
> *I am going. Beauty is all around me.*

That song is part of my DNA. That it would echo in the back of my brain is not surprising. What *is* surprising is that Caroline is the one humming it.

I blink back into focus for a minute, my fingers spread over the thread. That's the song, alright. Caroline doesn't know the Navajo, of course, but she does know the rhythm, which makes sense because she was there, holding the phone to Gam's ear when she sang it to me as she died.

The sound of it, even without the words, is enough to wash my mind clear.

And more than that, the spark isn't guttering anymore. It's still very much in danger, but it's not in *snippable* danger any longer. It's been knit back together just a little bit—not much, but enough to ease the pressure of the oncoming veil.

Caroline stops humming, lost in her own goodbye, and the spark gutters again.

"Keep humming!" I blurt, even going so far as to try to grab her shoulder and shake her back out of a goodbye that doesn't have to happen, but my hand just passes through her body. "Caroline! It's the song!"

She has to hear me. She has to be *made* to hear me. *But how?* My mind races.

"Hey!" I scream. "Caroline! Keep humming!"

She tilts her head a little, maybe sensing my movement but not my voice. I might as well be screaming from the bottom of the ocean.

The spark fades. "No, no, no," I say, trying to cup it myself, willing the veil away again, feeling nothing at all, ever—until I do.

My hand catches on something—not Caroline and not the spark, even.

The feather.

I bat it right from her hands.

For a second, both of us are so stunned that we just watch it float to the ground.

Caroline breaks the silence because, of the two of us, I'm the one that hasn't been able to do a damn thing in the living world for as long as I can remember, and I'm the one that would likely have stood like a deer frozen in the headlights until Dark Sky broke the world open.

"Ben?" she asks, a question that is everything in a name.

But she looks hurt. And I realize now that the feather was helping to protect the spark. And while the feather is good—it has some of Chaco's power, after all—it's not what is gonna save her child. The song will save the child.

So I do the only thing I can think of. I pick up the feather and press it to the desert dirt, and I write two words: "Keep singing."

It feels so damn good to hold something with weight, to make myself heard in the land of the living. I throw up a fist in thanks to Chaco. Even gone, he is the gift that keeps on giving. The only reason I can hold it is because this feather, much like the bird it belonged to, existed on all planes.

If he was here right now, I know he would be doing his little head bob of joy when Caroline starts humming Gam's song again. Not me, though—I just watch, vision watery, as the spark grows stronger again.

"The song," she says, her own tears dripping off her chin, patting softly into the fabric of her shirt. "It's the song."

"It calls on the power of this place," I say aloud, putting everything together in my own head. "It's the key."

She can't hear me, but she realizes it the same time I do, and both of us look up the mountain. That's what Gam was aiming to do: to sing the song at the anchor, to knit the break back together, and to seal it with the feather.

She pauses her humming and holds out the feather. "Take it, Ben. Give it to them. Tell them."

But I push it gently back. That's the only way I can think to tell her that if I take that feather into the soul map, it might never come back. It might melt into the same soul soup Chaco disappeared into, and all will be lost.

"We're going to lose them all without you," I say, and I cup the feather so that I can almost make myself feel like I'm holding her hand—almost. "Please help them, Caroline."

What I don't add, even to the dead air in which I speak, is *and me too. Help me. Because this is all my fault, and if I have to escort them across the veil today, I do believe what's left of my mind will be blown to pieces.*

My words can't reach her, but she understands. She always did. We never really needed words. She grips the feather, and she hums Gam's song, and she reaches for her crow.

She does what Caroline does best. She rolls up her sleeves and walks straight into the storm.

22

OWEN BENNET

The thin place finally caught me for good. I walked right into it, an idiot fly thinking he knew his way around this spider's web. *Ironic.* We doctors think often about what aspect of ourselves will finally be the one to fail, the one that sets in motion that great unbalancing that ultimately lays low the body itself. I had odds on my liver. "Soul freezing in the land between life and death" wasn't even in the running. But here we are.

The blinding brightness of the vortex somehow makes the cold burn worse. Nothing that bright should be this cold. I can't even look at it. All I can do is pull at these chains of white smoke, yanking again and again for purchase with my feet and clawing blindly with fingers that are quickly losing all feeling. All my efforts have no effect. What looks like smoke holds like cement, with no give whatsoever. It's as if the white smoke has burrowed under the skin, lumpy and undulating, wrapping tighter.

Joey is here, too, fighting for me. God bless him. The roar of the spirit wind is so loud that I can't talk to him, nor him to me. But I feel his grip around my hand, trying to pry my fingers away from the crow totem. He was always the strongest of all of us in this place, but even he has to phase in and out before the smoke traps him too. I try to tell him to leave me, to take care of Caroline and Grant, but he keeps coming back, keeps trying.

A shadow passes over the vortex, and both of us chance a glance. The thin form of Kai appears, kneeling down and reaching awfully close to the break. Her hand crosses the plane, and it takes on that same sick brightness. The thin place is loud, roaring, but I can still hear her scream. A scream like that elicits an almost Pavlovian response. Joey reaches out to her, as do I. She's clearly in pain, but she still presses her hand forward.

Then, horrifically, she leans down and starts pressing the crown of her head through too. The break is small, but so is Kai. If she wants to stick her head in whatever guillotine this is, she can do it.

I sense more movement, and Grant is there, following her, his form a roaring gauze of sepia when seen from this side. I yell for him to get away because this is exactly what Dark Sky wants, but my scream is ripped from my numb limps and scattered to infinity.

Grant reaches for her, and the bell bumps up against the vortex with a flash that's nuclear bright, a new burn on top of the cold, a humbling pain. I have to shut my eyes again and turn away, but I've seen all I need to. The bell is a key, and the vortex is a door, and it is doing its job. The break is widening, and I'm about done.

Strangely, in this roaring, unnatural place where a full-throated scream can barely be heard, I catch a few notes of a song, a humming. Something so soft and gentle should be wiped out here, but instead, it grows stronger. And as it grows, the cold lessens.

Caroline. My ears hear her, but my soul recognizes her first—the feel of her nearby, her warm hands on either side of my head, her forehead to mine, thawing me. I yank my hand and feel the smoke give a little. Joey feels it too. He pulls, and I pull, and Caroline hums, and I feel the smoke snap and recoil. I drop my crow and drop hard into reality, on my back, sucking in life-giving warmth. I want to hug the rocks, lick the dirt, eat the air. But we have no time for that, not if I want to save Grant.

I try to pick myself up and run to where he's trapped at the break, pulling at Kai even as the thin place pulls at the bell, but I stumble, legs still numb. No matter—if I can't walk, I'll crawl. Caroline is here, still humming, and I can't make myself look at her because then I'll see that our baby is gone. That little spark has paid the price for us. I won't see the smoke, but I'll see it on her face nonetheless, loud and clear. And I can't take that. But she makes me. She helps me stand and looks me straight in the eye, and I see acceptance there, a type of wisdom I've never seen before. I don't know what it means, but it gives me hope.

She turns to Joey, still rubbing his own burn away, and holds out the feather. "Gam's song," she says. "Sing it with everything you've got left."

Joey looks at the feather wide-eyed. I have no idea what she's talking about, but thankfully, Joey seems to. Recognition dawns on him, and he picks up where Caroline left off but with words. I can't understand the Navajo, but I don't need to understand to feel the power in the words. They seem amplified by this place, as if each is a stone, adding to the substance of the mountain, patching it back together.

Joey sings more loudly. He thumps his chest with the fist in which he's clasped the feather. He stomps his feet to the driving drumbeat of the song, and in a definite moment, the song crosses over to become a chant, a call, an order.

I feel it calming the wind.

Just as I allow myself to think we might get off this mountain in one piece, something else catches my ear. A higher sound, raking, clashes with Joey's chant.

Jacob Dark Sky crests the stairs, belting his Windway chant as if he's been singing the entire way from the trading post to the mountain. He's leading a long line of followers, and the dark wind rises again.

23

THE WALKER

D ark Sky may be singing the song, but I am the reason the dark wind is ripping through the thin place and into the land of the living. It's my fault—not what I did but what I didn't do.

I forgot who I was.

I became the Walker and left Ben forever behind, spreading myself thin over all the living souls of the world.

I became a faceless cloud with a scythe, a mere tool for the veil. I lost my own anchor. I bet it started as no big deal. I probably allowed myself to fog over one or two memories here and there, to zone out during one or two tough jobs—just the flutter of a butterfly wing. And now the storm has hit: Grant, about to throw himself past the point of no return after Kai, who might already be there, half in and half out of two worlds, and Hosteen, going to meet Dark Sky, joining in a chant that likely hasn't been sung since Wind used it to crack open the second world and lead the Air Spirit people away.

The song is the sound of the sky breaking.

All Dark Sky needs to do is look at a thing, and his blind eyes rip into it, changing it, conforming it, opening it up.

Tendrils of white, now as thick as my arm, brace either side of the vortex and pull. Bits of the living world crumble to the ground like eggshell, and the sepia whirlwind that is the thin place is revealed.

When Ana and I met and she passed the torch to me, she said, "It's a hard thing you go to do." I was so high on seeing her again, even for an instant, that I sort of filed that away in the back of my mind, but she was right. Boy was she right. She was only six years into the job then and ready to float that river to peace. I'm about to lap her. *And what do I have to show for it?* My home is breaking down. My people are fleeing.

Joey's singing puts up a good fight. Gam's spirit power packs a punch. It always has and always will, but that's not enough to stop our people from going, not if they want to go. Kai is there at the break, beckoning, and they come.

One by one, they duck under, in, and through, and as each leaves, I feel it. I feel a part of this land being chipped away just as the wind wears down the mountain. And the way they look at Dark Sky as they pass, the grateful desperation in their eyes, breaks my heart.

I see them as they go, and I remember them. The Nageezy kids, boys when we used to play kick the can with them, are all grown now. Shilah Yazzie limps through after his father, with Jonah Nez, too, who gave me my first cigarette—three, actually, traded for some leftovers I stole, of Gam's chicken posole. I coughed myself blue after half of the first one, and Joey snapped the rest and tossed them into a fire.

These are Arroyo people, mostly. I know them. Each

that bends their way through puts a piece of my memory back in place, setting my past right, which anchors my present.

Chooli Running Water walks through, the only constant rock left of her clan. Her soul thread says she's sixty-two, but her body is at least a decade older. You can see it in her stoop and the way her face droops with that kind of tiredness that no amount of sleep can fix. That's what happens when someone gives and gives. She tried to hold together a broken family—two of her own kids walked right off the Navajo Way. One huffed himself to death in a paint bag, and the other got into a head-on with a semi on I-70 in a stolen truck. She was never the same again.

Others pass, too, with no hogan to speak of but the Arroyo. Maria Bodaway walks through with her hands clasped behind her back, not a second's hesitation. I remember now that I showed up at the Bodaway trailer a few years back and picked up two of her three grandchildren at once, blasted from the world by Fentanyl-laced heroin. The third lingered for a bit at the CHC before I picked him up too.

There goes Yas Hathali, one of Maria's cousins who lived across from her at the Boxes. He does look back but not for long. He's as set on leaving as the rest of them. No drug deaths have taken the Hathalis so far, just cards and liquor, the two oldest bullets in the book. I remember the council blackballed him and his brother Atsa from the Wapati casino when I was still in high school. Somehow, Atsa got a marker for more than he would ever make in a year by staking what was left of his eighteen money, and he lost it in one day. The tribe giveth, and the tribe taketh away. That night, he drank himself into oblivion with bootleg liquor and walked out into the winter without a coat or even shoes. I escorted him across not long after.

The Smoker! The gatekeeper for the Arroyo is the one who held vigil over Oka Chalk's totem pile when he died, the one who helped translate the stories of the elder twins.

"You can't leave!" I say. "The elder twins need you! The Arroyo needs you!"

He doesn't even look back when he steps through.

Everything is coming together now, as so many things do, only when we're losing them. Ten, twenty, thirty brothers and sisters are gone, one by one. Joey is holding the feather high and singing with tears streaming down his face. Grant is trapped with his neck in the noose, grasping for Kai, who is both here and there, living proof that pain does exist where these people are going. At the threshold, she strains like she's holding it open herself.

Joey is faltering. He holds the feather like it's a lodestone. His arms shaking, he marks each loss with his eyes shifting left to right like he's counting the beads on an abacus. Chooli and a bunch of the other Running Waters live ten or so cars down from him. The Nageezy boys live —or lived—across the way. These people are his neighbors, his friends.

The feather lowers. Caroline leans against him, closing her eyes, humming. Owen is trying to pull Grant back, and I can see he's thinking about phasing again if that's what it takes.

In short, we've lost.

But if I have to lose, I want to lose like my Gam did, singing my people away.

I walk over to Joey and stand face-to-face with my oldest and best friend, and I clasp both hands around the feather, and I sing. I put all the names to all the faces and all the places that make up my Dinétah, and I sing it the way Gam did. I sing farewell.

> *I am going in freedom.*
> *I am going, I am going,*
> *I am going in beauty.*
> *I am going, I am going,*
> *I am going. Beauty is all around me.*

I can hold only the feather, not my friend, not today. But the feather is what's heavy today, and Joey senses my grasp instantly. His eyes snap open, searching, sweeping over me but still recognizing.

"Help me, brother," he whispers. "Help me close this."

Together, hand in hand, we raise the feather higher. I hold my people in my head, each a missing puzzle piece in my mind, and as each piece clicks, the wind dies a little more.

Right away, I know Dark Sky doesn't like that one bit. His chant dries up, his face turning ugly as he grabs Hosteen.

"Quickly," he snarls. "Get them through."

Hosteen looks lost, over his head, but he's always been a stubborn ass, and he's not about to turn back now. He pushes Kai through the unraveling with one hand, and I watch, helpless, as Grant follows, dragged by his own refusal to let her go.

I know enough about the thin place to know that once they're inside, they're gone. All it takes is a step to disappear. Owen knows it, too, and he slams the full whip-strength of his lanky frame into Hos from the ground up. His shoulder connects at Hosteen's neck, and both fly through the unraveling into the thin place. Kai and Grant tumble in afterward. The bell lights up with the fire of the desert sun and pulses once with a visible sound wave that passes through the portal and flattens everyone, me included.

Dark Sky steps through, last in the line, and as he does, he starts to transform.

That hellish white smoke wraps his face in an insect mask. White antennae sprout, wisplike, from his head. More smoke pours down his body, layering itself heavy and milk-white into twitching wings that waterfall down his back as he stands tall, a creature of shifting smoke, one of the ancient Air Spirit people come alive again.

He stretches and sighs with contentment. He turns toward the unraveling and bends his neck to look through, antennae seeking. "When I have the bell, this doorway will be open to all Diné forever," he says with infuriating calm, in the exact same booming voice as Jacob Dark Sky. "And believe me when I say they will come. If not now, then soon. Eventually, the call will be too strong to ignore."

His tendrils sweep out over the broken people who followed him, and as they are touched, the burn of the thin place seems to lessen. They become more docile, forming up in a line, as if to continue their march. A quick check of their threads shows that while the colors have been bleached and their story is impossible to read, the integrity still stands. These people will not die here as long as they have Dark Sky's touch.

Grant gets no such protection.

The pain of the thin place is already needling him. He struggles to breathe. He's turning a different kind of white, a dead kind.

Dark Sky watches with his bloodless gaze, waiting with Hosteen by his side. "This is how you hand it to me, Keeper. When the Walker escorts you to the river beyond. All I have to do is pick it up. The key to the next world will be mine."

Grant is too weary to fight. He's beaten down, burned out by the job. I know that feeling. Under other circumstances, if he still had the same strength in his soul as he did when he was eight, he'd probably find a way to break Dark Sky's hold. But that child is gone. He's a man now, one that has been carrying a heavy thing for most of his life. And it's taken a toll.

I look to Joey, like I always used to when I had no idea what to do, but he's just searching for me. Without Gam's song pushing back against Dark Sky, the wind is rising again. But if we do sing, somehow managing to close the vortex, we'll lose the people of the Arroyo on the other side. We can save the Rez at the cost of its heart, at the cost of ripping my friends apart.

Owen's face falls, and he spins that old beaded bracelet around his wrist a few times. That's twice now Dark Sky has hit at his family. But rather than start swinging, like I would've done—starting with that prick Hosteen Bodrey, who could use a few to the face—he kneels down by Grant and puts an arm around his son.

"Let's get out of here," he says softly, as if they were doing nothing more than bouncing from the local greasy spoon.

He sees all too clearly what I'm only now coming around to. As long as Dark Sky keeps Grant here, he wins. The power is in Grant's hands and always has been. Part of Grant is reaching for Kai, gently grasping her arm. But his other hand is gripping the bell like a noose around his neck, and that's what Owen sees.

I kneel down to the other side of him and speak before I have any chance to second-guess.

"Let it go, Grant."

I don't expect to be heard, don't expect anything more than to be the ghost I always am, but something, some whisper, seems to reach him. Maybe it's the fact that he's split between worlds, balancing on the bell. Maybe it's the fact that Chaco was his brother just as he was mine.

Or maybe it's that his mom comes up behind me, then to me, then through me, and in an instant, I can see in her face that she and I are of the same mind.

"This is not the end," Caroline says. "Everything comes around again."

Those are Chaco's words, but not like Chaco said them, not like I've held them in my mind. The way she says it, the old phrase rings with hope.

Grant swallows hard then smiles. It's a sad smile, but it breaks the spell. That's what he needed, his mom saying it's okay to let it go.

He takes the bell off. He hands it to Dark Sky, and in an instant, the smug satisfaction of a plan well executed is wiped from him. I can see it in the way he backs up, antennae twitching.

Grant's face is contorted with grief, but his voice is rock-solid. "Careful what you wish for."

Dark Sky looks strangely at the bell, mandibles clicking. Joey starts to sing again, and the vortex begins to close. Owen looks at Grant, and his meaning is plain: *You get out first.*

But he's not the only one. Kai Bodrey looks at Grant too. For the first time since Dark Sky poisoned her mind, her eyes seem clear. Maybe Grant's selflessness stunned some life back into her.

I wasn't there for the history of these two. That's one of the things I missed in my fog. But a guy like me can read a lot in the thread that connects them on the soul map. It's delicately woven when it comes to letting go. Kai seems to have thought it meant one thing for a long time: getting out and starting new.

But now, as she looks at Grant, their shared thread is changing. Something is shifting her perspective. Maybe she's learning that "starting new" and "giving up" are two sides of the same coin, a bit too close for comfort. I can't blame her for struggling with that balance. I'm still trying to figure it out myself.

She slowly drops to her knees and crawls toward him, and he stops rubbing at his newly freed neck long enough to hold out a hand again, breathless hope in his eyes and dripping down his soul thread with the rich color of honey.

She slows, unsure. The problem isn't Dark Sky's pull so much as the way her heart is tied up with her shithead brother. Abuse sucks like that. Sibling blood is strong, even when half of it has gone bad. She still feels like she's abandoning him.

She grasps for Grant and utters something I think might be new for her. It's something I can't see anywhere in her thread, something foreign.

"Help me," she whispers.

And Grant does. He pulls her, gently at first, then when he knows she's on board, he pulls with more force until both of them tumble back out into the land of the living, their cold skin smoking in the blasting morning sun.

Owen follows right after, his thin frame nicking the shrinking walls as he dives through. The last of the vortex clips his shoe as he slides free on the sand of Knifepoint, then it's gone. Joey's voice is all that can be heard. As he lowers the feather to the gap, his song now sounds of mourning, of farewell.

I grasp the feather from the other side, and together, we seal it in the gap of Knifepoint. The turquoise clicks with the sound of a lock snapping shut. As it settles, the aquamarine color of the stone melts and spreads until it's the same dusty red as everything else. The rock is seamless once more. The anchor is whole.

The wind drops entirely. The feather seesaws slowly to the mesa floor. All of us stand in silence. The blue sky above feels very close and spreads out over the cliff like a vast, still ocean where we float, marooned.

But at least we're together.

Almost together, that is—we're missing one very important member of the crew. All that's left of Chaco is that feather, and I think the rest of the party is so stunned at the sudden stillness that nobody but me sees it smoking, slipping away one black thread at a time, now that its job is done.

Something about that doesn't sit right with me, so I do what I always do when I don't know what I'm doing or feeling. I just do something—anything.

I grab the feather and eat it. I swallow it just like I swallowed the whole bird. And my mind is blasted away once more into my grandmother's past and into my own.

24

MANABA MORNING ROCK

My granddaughter is dying. I have to tell myself this over and over again even as I sit knitting at her bedside, surrounded by the foul smells of the white man's medicine at the Albuquerque hospital where she will breathe her last breath. I tell it to myself because it is the only way I can come close to convincing myself that what I must do is right.

Nothing can save Ana now, not the white man's medicine, not the Diné medicine. She is beyond all of it. My son knows it. Sitsi knows it. Even my grandson knows it. I can tell by the way they walk in and out of the room for no reason, as if the truth was a bear here, waiting, one they can't stand for long.

I feel the bear, too, but I am too old to sit then stand, come then go. I knit to run away. And right now, I knit next to my granddaughter, who is dying. The two of us are the only ones in this cold, hissing, beeping room, so far from our people's hogan.

This isn't right. But it is what it is.

The only one who doesn't seem to know that she is

dying is my granddaughter herself. Our bodies are strange like that. We lie to ourselves. We lie especially when a truth as huge as the Black Bear begins to awaken.

Our people are built to survive, to struggle, to stay. Going is a hard thing to take, especially for a child of nine. She watches the sun play with a dream catcher that hangs above the window facing the east—always the east and the sun. At least this room has that.

Her breath is shallow. Her beautiful copper skin is gray. This disease of her heart has somehow eaten away at her face too. She is sunken, but when the dream catcher spins in the freezing air of this place and the sunlight plays with it, she still smiles. She looks at things as though she will still be looking at them tomorrow.

So it is up to me, then. I can see no path where what I am to do will not rip my family to pieces. They will not understand. But then, they cannot. The dream catcher spins in a wind made by man, but another wind still rages outside, one that Blackfeather still recovers from, one that nearly took him away from me, and one that is not done with my people just yet.

Because I failed to close the unraveling at Knifepoint, the wind grows. It will eventually take all my people then all those beyond the Dinétah unless I act.

For a time after my failure, I mourned. When the Walker has turned his face from this place, the wind cannot be calmed. And when the wind cannot be calmed, the anchor cannot be closed by any force in the land of the living. All was lost. What comfort I found came from the song I sang over and over again while I knitted. I sang for myself. I sang to ease Blackfeather's pain.

But mostly, I sang because it drowned out the truth that still spoke to me in the back of my mind, the truth

Blackfeather shared when I broke down at Knifepoint: there is another way.

Two truths: One—the Walker has turned his face from his people. Two—my granddaughter is dying.

Two more truths: One—fighting the dark wind without the Walker is futile. Two—my granddaughter's death need not be.

If the Walker has left this land for reasons known only to a creature ancient by any way of measuring time, then perhaps it is the duty of the Keeper to replace the Walker.

I pause in my knitting, and in the absence of the steady click of my needles, the hiss and moan of the room rings with terrible clarity. The time has come for an old woman to stand. But just as I grip the chair to brace myself, the door opens.

Joseph Flatwood enters with none of the fear of my own family but all the sadness. He acknowledges the Black Bear with a glare then turns toward me.

"My turn, grandmother," he says, speaking Diné, using the honorific as though we were blood. At this point, we might as well be. "You go get some rest. I will sit by her side."

He is stilled only when he turns toward Ana. Then he is as lost as the rest of us, a fourteen-year-old boy again, brittle, close to breaking.

"Joey!" Ana says or tries to say, but her breath won't quite push the name out like she wants. Still, she doesn't seem to care. She thinks that tomorrow might be better.

Joey's eyes swim with the knowledge we all share, that it will not. But he is strong, and he manages to keep them to a swim and not a pour. I do too, mostly.

"How do you feel, little one?" he asks, sitting on the

stool at her side and grasping her bird-claw hand gently in his.

"I feel... strange," she says. She drifts and looks at the dream catcher. This is as close as she's likely to get to understanding what the bell around my neck has been telling me for hours.

The time is very close.

What will happen will rip the Dejooli clan to pieces. We need not bring the Flatwood line into things.

"Joseph," I say quietly, meaning to find a way to let him say goodbye then leave, but he has no mind for me.

He grasps Ana's hand with his other also, cups it, and kneels to the ground as though in prayer.

"Is there anything I can do?" he asks, his voice a whisper, and I know he's asking her, but he's also asking me in that way he has that hints at an understanding that goes well beyond any other fourteen-year-old boy, his best friend included.

I pause. There is one thing he can do, something that might allow me to piece together my family after I break it apart.

But it will cost him dearly.

He turns his gaze slowly from Ana to me. He has been coming to her bedside diligently for months. He knows as well as I what is coming. We have spoken, first around the edges then more to the point. He knows. And he knows the Black Bear is stretching, walking toward us, ready to eat.

"Much will be broken," I say, whispering in Diné. "I cannot break you as well."

His response is immediate. "The only thing that can break me is knowing I did not do everything I could for my people." He swallows hard and looks down at Ana before adding, "For my family."

Ana looks up at him with a questioning smile. She understands some Diné, but not enough. In time, she would have. In time, she would have spoken beautifully and sung beautifully too. All she needed was time, but that is what she did not receive.

"I cannot tell you all of what you seek to know. And for that, you will be hated, reviled for your silence. You may even be banished. Do you understand?" I ask.

Joseph nods, still smiling sadly down at Ana, who is now slowly and silently struggling to breathe. The Black Bear has a tricky way of sneaking up when you're not looking.

I push myself to stand and walk over to my grand-daughter, who is dying. I sit on the bed, and Joseph steps away.

"Granddaughter," I say, speaking simply and clearly in Diné she will understand. "I think your time in this world is coming to an end."

She looks up at me and wrinkles her tiny nose, pouting a bit in such an innocent and clear understanding that I can no longer keep the swimming inside. Her breath rattles, and she has a hard time even holding her head up, but she still reaches toward my tears. She has never seen me cry. She was never meant to.

"I have to ask you for a gift," I say. "I failed to help our people. But there is a way that you can."

She mouths words that only rasp. She nods weakly instead.

I wish I had more time to explain, but even if I had the entire length and breadth of time of our people in my grasp, she could never understand, not until she sees.

"The Black Bear is almost here. The one we told stories about."

I see fear in her face for the first time, real fear. And I press my head to hers, to give her my strength, whatever I have left.

"You don't need to be afraid of him. He is ancient Diné, one who has lost his way. And his time is over."

She seems to have stopped breathing. I vaguely hear Joseph weeping behind me. I reach inside my shirt and pull out the bell. I take it from around my neck and hand it to her, placing the lanyard between her fingers so that she holds it like a blossom.

"When the Black Bear gets here, he will ask you to come with him."

Ana blinks as machines beep and lights flash. None of that matters.

"And when he does," I say, "you must answer no, and you must ring this bell. Can you do that?"

She can barely move her fingers, and I can no longer clearly see her through my tears, but her eyes flash—my granddaughter still.

The room blares. Beeps turn into horrible, solid strings of sound. And I am forced to do what I dread.

I stand. "We will meet again, Granddaughter, on the far side of the river. I love you now and forever."

I turn away then and walk to the door, pausing briefly by Joseph's side.

"Hard times come for you, Joseph Flatwood. But always remember, you are Diné, one of the great." I take the crow feather and turquoise fetish, Chaco's gift to the elder twins, passed to me, and I hand it to Joseph. "For strength," I say.

He shudders with sobs, but he nods and takes it.

And that is where I leave them, the two, together in the room.

I walk down the hall, away from my people, even as strangers rush past me with machines, trying to forestall the inevitable.

Before they can reach the door, the bell rings. The peal is so clearly not from this world that it is felt more than heard. Everyone within earshot is stunned without quite knowing why.

The swap has been made. The Black Bear has been banished. My gorgeous granddaughter has stepped into his place.

I make my way to the waiting room and collapse into a chair just as all the doctors and nurses burst through the door into her room.

They will be confused when they find her gone and Joseph Flatwood alone.

My blood family will be confused when they find Joseph Flatwood silent. Then they will be angry then heartbroken, my grandson most of all.

Joseph Flatwood will be forever changed. He might go his whole life searching for answers I cannot provide.

But it is done. I can feel it in my bones. The wind has been clipped, like a blanket thrown over a flame. There is a new Walker. We are at peace, for a time.

All there is left to do is mourn.

25

THE WALKER

The living memory ends, and I feel like I'm tossed from the bed of a moving truck. I tumble and reel, swallowed by vertigo, until I steady myself with both hands on the rock plateau of Knifepoint. The ground is solid and affirming even if my touch leaves no mark in the strewn sand.

No time has passed in the living world. Owen is still checking Kai's vitals. Caroline soothes vitals of a different sort, using her sight. Grant looks stunned, both at what he's gained in Kai and at what he's lost in the bell. Joey is checking the anchor, pushing gently here and there.

The living world holds true again. The Dinétah has been knit strong, back to what it was before all this, unchanged on the outside.

Inside, I'm reeling.

Everything comes around again. Ana's loss has layers that even I couldn't have guessed, and it's come around again, full circle. Gam knew this, and Chaco knew this. Gam lived the rest of her life knowing she'd sent Ana to do the Walker's work. I'm surprised by the wave of anger I feel washing over me. Unclenching my jaw requires conscious effort. Sure, Ana was going to cross over anyway, and sure, she would do whatever she could to help our people, but she was a *child*, for God's sake, a nine-year-old sent to do a job that came very close to burning out my own sanity. And she never told me, never told Joey.

As fast as it arrives, the anger fades. The fact is Gam was given an opportunity to fix things. Ana was on her way out. She made a choice nobody should ever have to make. I know nothing about the Walker that Ana replaced, except that he was an Athabascan man, ancient in every way, and he was going mad.

Gam knew that and more. She knew that in this gig, if madness sets in, things that should be anchored start to spin. Cracks appear. Winds that should be quiet start to blow.

She did what she had to do. She bought us time, another generation, trusting that when things came around again as they always do, we might have pieces in place then, people in place to patch the unraveling for good. And she was right.

But she didn't know the full story. She thought the Athabascan, this Black Bear, was a bad man, maybe crazy from the start.

I wonder what she would think if I told her he was very probably a simple farmer settling the plains or perhaps a medicine man of some sort, maybe a chief, but in all likelihood a normal man, a good man.

The job turned him.

I know because it almost happened to me. And if I'm not careful, it still can.

Losing your mind doesn't have to look like the common room in a psych ward. It's not usually babbling, rocking, wide-eyed lunacy. Sometimes, losing your mind is just that—losing it. Memories are slowly lost to fog. The foundations of your identity—the people and places—fade away, associations lost, history forgotten.

I had to watch my people walk away one by one before the fog cleared for me. Maybe this Black Bear had no such shock, no such trials. Maybe he just did his job until he just sort of lost it, until the only way to get through to him was to yank him off stage—Ana in, Black Bear out.

I've often wondered what that moment will feel like when I'm replaced. It's a moment I'm terrified of and one I've longed for at the same time. Now, I think maybe that moment should come sooner than later. The fog is clear as long as I ground myself in my people, making it a point to remember their faces and places. But the fog will return. I don't think anything can help that. Then the question becomes a matter of timing. I want to stay long enough to help but leave before I start ripping open worlds without knowing it.

The thought of hurting the people I love without knowing I'm doing it terrifies me. It makes me want to start looking for a replacement today. *But who's to say another would be any better?* At least I know the stakes now —unlike Black Bear, unlike Ana.

No, for better or for worse, I need to stick around for a little while longer. For one, we don't have the bell. I'm not going anywhere without it, like it or not.

Two, we need to save the Arroyo. And I don't mean the canyon full of trash back on the Rez either. The Arroyo has always been its people, and its people were stolen. I think I'd like to have a few words once we find them and see if the grass is greener or if, like Gam believed, maybe we're all better off taking a stand in the world we've got.

I got a few words I'd like to share with Jacob Dark Sky too—some words I'd like to share with my fist if I get the chance. I don't care if he's a god or an ancient or somebody's creepy witch uncle from way out west or all of them combined—he's gonna answer for what he's done.

I can sense them, these pilgrims between worlds. Dark Sky's magic is strong, and the trail is faint, but I've got a pretty wide reach and a few tricks still up my sleeve. With a little help—and a lot of luck—maybe we can find them.

But I don't want to stop Dark Sky just yet.

If we catch him now, we only treat the symptom. If we follow him, he'll lead us to the true puppet master. Then maybe we can root out the cause.

I've noticed some things.

I should have put two and two together the second I saw Dark Sky's totem. Clearly, it had power. Clearly, it was significant to him. If I'd come across that scene at the bootlegger camp back in my old cop days, ripping through Dark Sky's whirlwind in a beat-up cop cruiser with Danny Ninepoint at my side, that would've been the first thing I noticed. Ninepoint would have cuffed Dark Sky in that forceful way of his, and I would've pulled that damn thing out of the fire.

Instead, Chaco pulled it from the fire. I was so ripped up by seeing Chaco flame out that I forgot all about what burned him up in the first place: the Black Bear totem.

It's been right there all along, in the memory Chaco showed me of Gam and the elder twins. *"Old Black Bear breathes heavy tonight."* I remember stories she used to tell Ana and me to get us to shut up and stop jumping across our little twin beds long enough to go to sleep. *"You'll wake Black Bear."*

Still, I missed it. The fog was thick. But it's burned

away for now, and in its place is an old NNPD cop who notices things.

My final vision of her memory sealed the deal—Gam telling Ana to be strong when Black Bear comes, to say no when he tells her it's time to go, to ring the bell.

She took Black Bear's place. She fired his ass the second that bell rang, and she stepped right in.

But that crazy old Athabascan didn't go.

Whatever that man became in the generations he walked this earth, snipping strings and ushering souls, he was strong enough to withstand the call of the river.

Black Bear is still here. Dark Sky is his chief. And from what I've seen of Dark Sky, Black Bear is pretty pissed off.

One look at the state of the Rez oughta tell you why. The people he left roaming the free plains in the hundreds of thousands, living in relative peace, are not the people he saw when Ana dropped the axe on him and the fog cleared. What he saw then was a people penned, given a stamp's worth of land, and told to make do. They were told this was their life now.

What he saw was struggle, pain, and more than a little suffering.

Now, Black Bear has taken it upon himself to start over, to remake. This, to my mind, is the same thing as unmaking. He took a cookie cutter to the heart of our people and spirited them away with Dark Sky as their guide. He promised a new world.

Conveniently, nowhere in all this have I heard talk of the true cost of leaving the Dinétah, the place designated by the gods as our home. Nowhere has he considered the cost of leaving this land.

The land between these four mountains is a shadow compared to what our Athabascan forefathers walked, but it's ours. The land is our people, and the people are the land. Dinétah is more than the dirt between mountains. It's the blood, sweat, and tears of every Navajo that fought with all they had to survive.

The land may have shrunk, but the power grew. Each Navajo that lives adds to it. What we have is like a pure shot of the Navajo Way if we can keep it. Instead of bailing on every world that doesn't quite work out for us, maybe it's time to stand and fight for the space we've carved out as our own.

No, Dark Sky didn't get into that. He just conjured up some nonsense and made promises and preyed on people too weak and scared and desperate not to fall into his hands. And he did it all at the bidding of Black Bear.

I'm gonna find them both, and when I do, we're gonna have a little bit of what Danny Ninepoint used to call "a straightening out."

First the bell, next the Arroyo. I don't know how, but I believe we can do these things.

The one thing I don't think I can do is turn toward Caroline to take in what I may or may not see in her thread.

What scares me most is what I might not see, a spark undone, an empty nest in the core of her soul.

The veil will tell me soon enough if I must take the spark away. When I help these souls-that-are-not-yet-human across, that's not a normal escort. With no bodies to speak of, they instead exist a little like fireflies. I cup them in my hand and carry them to the veil, then I softly blow them across. The veil is as gentle in the taking as I am in the giving. I've done this so many times—more than you'd ever believe—but each one hits me hard. *And this one...*

So no, I'm not gonna look yet. Instead, I'll sit right here on the edge of Knifepoint and follow all the birds that are coming back, wheeling round and round in the updrafts, spiraling through the bright-blue desert sky. And I'll think of Chaco.

26

CAROLINE ADAMS

Owen embraces me. I fit so neatly into his arms, chin to shoulder, that no space lies between us. His pulse hammers in my ears. His skin is still thawing, but his back is warm, blasted by full sun. It feels incredible.

The spirit wind has dropped entirely. In its place, a soft breeze blows across the living land, bringing with it the sounds and smells of the desert, things that are returning. Owen's smoke is stilled, so quiet that he's too terrified to ask the question I know is on his mind, too terrified to even think it.

I could look down at the place where the flicker sparked in me, but I don't need to, not anymore.

It's there. I can feel it growing even now, feel it amplified through Owen, its heat spreading through his lower back where he's pressed against me. The flicker knows.

But Owen doesn't, not yet.

"We're all still here," I whisper.

Owen pulls slightly away, looks down, eyes already alight. "All of us?"

"All of us," I say. And I pull him in again.

27

GRANT ROMER

She's back—here, with me, resting against my shoulder. I can hardly believe it. I keep one arm around her to remind myself she's real.

Kai is here, but she ain't quite right.

The sun has burned away the cold of the thin place in the rest of us, but Kai still shivers. Dad tells me it's just freeze burn, that she was in there longer than anyone without protection had any right to be, but I don't think that's all there is to it.

A new kind of loss dims her eyes. Her gaze lingers a bit too long. She takes a while to process what I'm saying, and when she does, even though her voice is her own, her attention seems split. Part of her is here—the part that asked for help, the part that scrambled back through to the land of the living—but part of her is gone. Maybe it's still wandering the thin place with her brother and the rest of the Arroyo, following Dark Sky through whipping sepia wind, numb to it all.

She comes back from the distance and finds me. Her eyes soften. "What now?"

"Wish I knew," I say, sitting up straight and dusting my hands on my jeans. "But I guess we can start by headin' back home."

The trek down to the lot is quiet. A single glance at Mom gets me a nod that she's okay, and Owen is okay, and my brother or sister is still okay in there. That, combined with the sun and the feel of Kai's hand in mine, settles over me like a blanket. I feel like I could fall asleep walking.

At the trailhead, we come upon a harsh reminder of what we've lost. Abandoned cars, trucks, and beat-up old RVs overflow the lot and snake down the shoulder leading in. Many seem parked in haste, haphazardly, bumper-to-bumper in a frozen ghost procession. The entrance is basically jammed, and I can already hear a few honks from the base of the turnoff. Hikers or sightseers are trying to get in now that the dark wind isn't keeping them away subconsciously.

I feel like tippin' over. Part of that is the exhaustion, now that we're stopped. But mostly, it's the bell, the lack of the bell. I guess I never really knew how much it kept me grounded until it was gone. Now, I feel like I'm floating. My balance is all out of whack. Kai seems to sense it, so she grabs my hand between both of hers, a different sort of anchor.

"I wish I could say I don't know what happened, what came over me. But I do," she says, low. "I wanted it. Wanted all of it until... until I didn't. Then it was too late."

"It's not too late," I say.

She wells up with tears that she quickly wipes away, which I think is a good sign. Tears spilling out means she's filling up again inside. "Our people are gone. The Arroyo is gone. The bell is gone."

"Nothing is really gone," I say. "Everything comes back around again. It's just a matter of how."

She looks at me with more questions than I have answers, and she shakes her head. "I'm so sorry, Grant. I never meant to hurt you or Caroline... Owen, Joey, none of you." She puts her head in her hands and rubs at her face like she's still waking up.

"I'll take that apology if you take mine for my people constantly trying to destroy everything your people were and are," I say, popping an eyebrow.

"That's ridiculous," she says, and there's that wry smile. "It wasn't you."

I reverse her grip on my hands, pressing hers between mine. "I have a hard time blaming you for wantin' better for your people. Although I do sometimes wonder why you think you can't find what you need right here."

My voice sort of crackles out at the end there. She gets my meaning. We had a plan. She was going to college in ABQ. I was gonna follow and get in with a good carshop, maybe start up as a mechanic. It wasn't much of a dream, but it was ours, and it worked in our heads. Or I thought it did, at least.

Kai looks at me, eyes wide pools of deep brown. "I don't know what I want," she says. "I think that was the problem. College doesn't seem right. Staying doesn't seem right. Every decision feels wrong except one."

I'm afraid to ask, but she leans into me and rests her head on my shoulder. Just like before, she doesn't need to speak. And I let out a huge breath I didn't know I was holding.

Joey is the one that brings us back to reality. Joey Flatwood, who can walk the thin world longer than anyone alive, is also the one most tied to the here and now, the realities we face. And I don't think that's a coincidence.

"What a mess," he says, looking at the cars. "We gotta move a fair number of these if we ever plan on going back to the Rez."

He turns to me and Kai. "Either of you know how to hotwire a car?"

"Of course I know how to hotwire a car," Kai says. "I'm Hos Bodrey's sister. He taught me how to hotwire a car for my tenth birthday. I shit you not. It was his present to me, he said."

Joey laughs, loud, and it's a wonderful sound. It breaks the strange silence that was threatening to settle in. "Well, just so happens I also know to hotwire cars. It was an... Arroyo thing." He looks back up at the way to Knifepoint and gives a nod that's much more than an acknowledgement of the past. It's a promise for the future.

"Let's start stripping wires," he says to Kai.

I also know how to hotwire a car, although not out of necessity, mostly out of wanting to understand engines, but I stay back. That floaty feeling is still strong, and I don't feel all that steady. I remember this feeling from when Pap died, and then Chaco. I feel this when things that make me feel solid and real disappear.

Mom and Dad look like they're catching the first breath of a new life. I don't want to break whatever peace they've found. I know better'n most how brief those moments can be. Instead, I decide to take a walk.

I don't plan to go far, but before I know it, the lot is gone, and even the raspy sound of engines sparking to life seems far away. My feet take me to the base of a newly felled piñon tree, which is strange, since as far as I know, it's been a bluebird summer day outside the thin place.

The tree is big, the splintering fresh. Sap drips in gold and green from wet wood that smells like a summer storm. It stood at the far edge of a steppe, where the vast blue of the sky flickers through the felled canopy. Its leaves will wilt and die now. I pluck one and rub it between my fingers and huff it. It's like the best smells of the Rez in a bottle.

I wanna go home.

I turn to go, but I hear something. People who don't live out here would probably think it's nothing more than a sigh of the wind, but I know better.

A snake is sliding through the underbrush.

Sandy diamonds glitter off its back, black and brown. I don't need to hear a rattle to know. It could be no other kind of snake—not in this place and not on this day.

It passes me by, going for the tree. I can hardly believe my luck. I used to be a target for these damn things when I had the bell, but not anymore. And I know I should get the hell along my way and leave good enough alone.

I take a few steps back toward the lot, but I stop and turn back. Just letting a snake on a mission go, without knowing what that mission is, doesn't sit right with me.

The trail is easy enough to see, a slow finger drag through the sand. It leads all the way to the fallen canopy and through it.

Then I almost get myself killed, of course.

I come right up on it, curled and ready to strike, but in a strange silence. The only thing that saves me is that it didn't expect me any more than I expected it.

The rattle fires loud, louder than normal, dirty coins in a metal can loud. It turns toward me and away from what it was going after, a birds' nest that fell to the ground with the tree.

It snaps at me, a halfhearted snap, but a halfhearted snap from a rattler is enough to make anybody jump back. Still, it doesn't want me. It wants the nest. Specifically, it wants the broken baby birds there. The fledglings are barely old enough to show a dusting of black coloring.

Crows.

The birds look dead, too small to have survived whatever hit this tree. Only an idiot goes after a rattlesnake the length of their leg over a nest of dead crows. As much as I hate to turn away, I'm gonna leave it be and let the damn thing eat, but as I do, I hear another sound. A little chirrup—then a rustle and another little chirrup.

I hang my head for a second. I guess not all of them died. One pokes its way out from underneath its still brothers and sisters. It falls awkwardly on the fine dust a few feet from the snake, which is slowly rising, priming and cocking itself.

The fledgling crow stands as tall as a tiny thing is able to and squares up, and maybe that's what makes me do it.

I step quickly, with no hesitation. The heel of my boot comes down clean and true, and I cut with the back edge, worn sharp by walking hundreds of miles of reservation. The snake had no chance. Its head pops off with the sound of a knuckle cracking and bounces away into the leaves.

Its thick body twitches a few times then stills. Blood seeps into the sand.

The crow chick chirrups once at the snake then turns toward me. For a second, we just look at each other. And now, I don't know if I'm dreaming or if I really did float away, because I'm thinking I see a bit of a red streak underneath the black fuzz on its tiny chest. It's faint, but it's real. And the crow chick is stumbling its way over to me.

I cup my hands, and it shuffles inside of them, and I lift it up.

I bring it to my eyeline and look at it, knowing I'm crying but not really feeling it and definitely not taking my eyes from this bird.

It stands as tall as it's able and stretches its little fledgling wings and says to me, "I think I know you."

The voice is soft and small in my mind, different but somehow familiar. I can't respond with anything more than a burst of laughter that's also sort of a sob.

I slowly bring my hand to my shoulder, and the little thing hops off, wobbly, until I help steady it in a space under my ear that seems like it was made for it.

"Chaco?" I whisper, not daring to look. "Is that you?"

It rustles. "I don't know," says the voice in my mind. "But that sounds about right."

I don't dare touch it though I want to. I don't know how baby birds work, but I don't want to hurt it. "I missed you, buddy."

I feel the rustle against my neck, more like a sigh this time. "Why?" Chaco asks.

It's a genuine question. He doesn't know or can't remember.

"Because I love you," I say. "And you had to go away. I thought I'd lost you forever."

The bird settles into me. "Nothing is lost forever," it says.

I know the second half of that one. He told it to me, once. Everything comes back around again, eventually— the bad and the good. I have a million questions, a million things I want to say. But all that seems too much for right now, for this moment.

Instead, I walk with my bird back to my family in a quiet that feels brand new.

AUTHOR'S NOTE

I started my own journey into the Chaco Reservation and all the magic and mystery it held almost a decade ago. In a flurry of inspiration, I wrote three books in two years, then I stepped away from the Vanished series. I'd always wanted to write more, feeling that the characters had so much more to say, but the right story didn't come my way. Until now.

The inspiration for this new story came from all over, including the land itself. If you've ever watched the sun set over the Sangre de Cristo Mountains, you know what I'm talking about. A few books in particular also helped fuel the fire for this story: The American Indian Mind in a Linear World, by Donald L. Fixico helped me work my way into the circular way of thinking. Hand Trembling, Frenzy Witchcraft, and Moth Madness, by Levy, Netra, and Parker is a heartbreaking and detailed medical study of Navajo seizure disorders that helped bridge some medical gaps. And, of course, the Diné Bahane', translated by Paul G. Zobrod. Wherever I reference the Navajo Creation Story, I took care to try and maintain as much accuracy as possible within the context of the story. I hope I succeeded.

I'd also like to give a shout-out to a very informative research paper I stumbled across by Hall, Flamming, and Usselman of the Georgia Institute of Technology's School of History, Technology and Society, called The Navajo Concept of Wind. Fascinating stuff.

Finally, to all the ardent fans who have waited patiently for this return, I just want to say thank you. Thank you for reading. Thank you for the kind emails and notes of support. Most of all, thank you for your patience. There is much more to come.

—BBG

ABOUT THE AUTHOR

B. B. Griffith writes best-selling fantasy and thriller books. He lives in Denver, CO, where he is often seen sitting on his porch staring off into the distance or wandering to and from local watering holes with his family.

See more at his digital HQ: https://bbgriffith.com

If you like his books, you can sign up for his mailing list here: http://eepurl.com/SObZj. It is an entirely spam-free experience.

ALSO BY B. B. GRIFFITH

Printed in Great Britain
by Amazon

20162398R00164